I'm

What Three Children Taught Me About
Embracing Emotions and Parenting

Fine

By Leonora Found

SUMMIT PRESS

Disclaimer: The information in this book is provided for entertainment, educational, and informational purposes only. The personal transformation stories, relationship advice, and decision-making strategies reflect the authors' personal experiences and professional opinions. What has worked for the author may not be suitable for every individual or situation.

Names, identifying details, and certain scenarios may have been changed to protect the privacy of individuals involved in the stories shared throughout this book.

Summit Press Publishers
PO Box 1356
Intervale, New Hampshire 03845

First Edition: 2026
ISBN: 979-8-9939104-0-6

For information about special discounts available for bulk purchase, workshops, retreats, and webinars associated with this book, please contact us at author@summitpresspublishers.com.

To Neil, Michaela, Matthew and Josh. Thank you
for helping me turn our chaos into chapters and
our growing pains into something resembling
wisdom. In the end, public processing was
definitely cheaper than therapy.

TABLE OF CONTENTS

Part III
Navigating School-Aged Emotions

Part IV
Navigating Teen Emotions

Part V
Navigating a Young Adult's Emotions

Part VI
Carrying It Forward

INTRODUCTION

Dear Kids,

I hope this letter finds you well.

Thank you for letting me be your mother. It has been an adventure, and I have grown in ways I never imagined possible. That said, I'm writing to let you know I'm officially resigning from the position, effective immediately. After years of faithful service, my emotional inbox is overflowing. I need to remember what it feels like to have a thought, maybe even a feeling, that doesn't require immediate triage.

From this point forward, I'll be available on a consulting basis. You may contact me for occasional support or urgent washing machine queries, but all other requests should be redirected to Dad. (Especially those beginning with "Where is…?")

I look forward to cheering you on from the sidelines.

With all my love and a mildly exhausted heart,

Mom

Of course, I didn't send that letter, but the idea was so satisfying that I gave it a proper write-up, just to see how I'd phrase it if it ever reached that point. Curious to test the waters, I pinned it to the fridge with a "Mother of the Year" magnet, which struck me as the perfect irony.

Did anyone notice or offer a half-hearted "You okay, Mom?" Not a word. The fridge swung open a hundred times, and not once did anyone seem the least bit curious. Point made.

What This Book Is About

To be clear, this isn't about quitting motherhood (though if LinkedIn ever adds "Former Parent" as an option, I might be tempted). This is about learning to tune into our emotions, and those of our children, before we hit the point of quietly wondering if stepping back would be easier than staying present.

Whether you are new to parenting or feel like you've been doing it long enough to qualify for a loyalty card, there's wisdom that comes from sharing stories, especially the ones where we admit we got it wrong and wonder what we'd do differently. That's what you'll find here: real stories drawn from years of growing alongside my children and their emotions. Some may make you laugh; some may make you cringe; and others, I hope, will make you quietly nod in recognition.

I don't share these because I've cracked the code on emotional regulation. I haven't. I share them because I know the relief of hearing someone else say, "Oh. . . it's not just me."

I'm not a parenting expert or a child psychologist. Let's be clear about that. I'm a mother with twenty-five years of scraped knees, school runs, teenage storms, and emotional growth that only comes from doing the work right alongside your children. What I've learned is that if we want our kids to feel safe with their emotions, we have to show them what it looks like to handle ours.

Some of what's helped me comes from my background in psychology and my work as a life coach, but most of it was learned in real time—in kitchens, cars, and late-night conversations. The ideas here aren't instructions but reflections that I hope will help you find your footing when the path feels unclear.

How I Got Here (and Why It Matters)

For years, I was the efficiency expert of motherhood, armed with systems and a kind of calm authority that pointed to someone who had their life together. But beneath that were layers of thoughts and feelings I barely had time to notice. I recall attempting to tap into my inner world during those drawn-out early reading sessions, but listening to a child sound out d-o-g that slowly is so quietly torturous it dissolves any chance of mental clarity before it even begins.

The truth is, ignoring feelings doesn't make them disappear. They just pile up quietly in a folder titled "Deal with Later."

My "lucky" children got the organised version of me, but not the real one. So, when my daughter told me she wished I could be "like other mothers," it hit hard. What she really meant was, *I want more of you, not more of your management.* And she was right.

What I didn't see then was that the cracks were tiny signs pointing me toward what really matters in family life. It wasn't about more activities or tighter systems. It was about shifting my focus from managing what was happening on the outside to noticing what was going on inside me and inside them.

It turns out there's a big grey area between keeping it all together and actually feeling it. That's where this started, in the middle. Somewhere in there, I began to learn that presence mattered more than perfection, and that connection only happens when you drop the performance and show up as yourself. Slowly, that started to soften the edges of our family life.

What's Waiting Inside

This book spans four distinct stages of parenting, each with its own emotional landscape.

1. Toddler years: emotions are loud, immediate, and involve a muffin meltdown
2. School-age: friendship drama, quiet hurts, and learning to read between the lines
3. Teenage years: identity storms, testing boundaries, and staying connected when they push away
4. Young adulthood: stepping back while staying close, holding space without holding control

But unlike so many other parenting books, this one isn't just about your child. It begins with the unseen emotional journey of motherhood.

5. Motherhood: shifting identity, quiet doubts, and why your growth is just as vital as your child's

Why All These Stages?

I've parented through them all. And if there's one thing I've learned, it's that what we teach our children early on about emotions—how to name them, hold them, and not fear them—threads through every stage that follows. It's also what keeps us grounded in the process.

You'll see that I didn't get it right straight away. Far from it. There were years of trial, error, and the occasional dramatic meltdown, quite often mine. But wherever you are in your parenting journey, you'll recognise the same emotional thread, the one that runs from toddler tantrums to those adult conversations that finally land.

Reading This Your Way

Parenting doesn't happen in neat chapters, and neither does this book. You don't have to read it in order or in a way that exactly matches your children's ages. Just begin where you are. Some days that might mean searching for perspective on a toddler's meltdown; other days, wrestling with a teenager's slammed door, or the quiet ache of watching a young adult pull away. Each part stands on its own, but they echo one another, because emotional growth doesn't move in straight lines. It loops, overlaps, and sometimes circles back.

If time is short, head to the "For Skim Lovers" at the end of each section; it will give you the essentials. When you're ready to explore more deeply, the stories will be there to meet you with honesty, humour, and the quiet reminder that none of us are walking this road alone.

An Invitation

At some point, you've probably found yourself thinking, *Am I even cut out for this?* Maybe it was while hiding in the bathroom for a moment's peace or pretending not to hear your name being called for the hundredth time that morning. Or maybe it was when your child, once glued to your side, suddenly doesn't want to talk to you.

If so, you're not alone. Those moments don't mean you're doing it wrong; they mean you care enough to wonder. Emotions aren't just a by-product of family life; they are the very fabric of it. When we explore them together, not as parents with all the answers, but as people learning together, something shifts. Family life becomes richer, more honest, and most definitely, more human.

This book is an invitation to explore that space between love and overwhelm, the place where presence meets honesty and where being real matters more than being right. It's about the small, human moments that shape us: the laughter, the mess, the misunderstandings, and the quiet repairs. Parenting will never be tidy, and "fine" will rarely mean what it says. Still, more often than not, when you stop bracing for disaster and start showing up as yourself, life feels a little more manageable. And where better to begin than with you.

Part I

Navigating a Mother's Emotions

FINDING MYSELF IN SOMEONE ELSE'S SCRIPT

I'm always struck by how quiet a house can feel when it's empty. No shrieks about missing shoes, no one staring into a full fridge insisting there's nothing to eat, and no voice shouting, "Maarrrrrm" about a lost rugby ball. Because obviously, that's what mothers do in their spare time, right? We lace up and head out for a quick game of neighbourhood rugby. A pleasant thought. But no.

When silence arrives, I leap up like a meerkat on espresso. *Free time! Let's alphabetise the spices,* as if sitting still might trigger an alarm.

For years, I told myself I was just wired differently. I didn't need rest. I was powered by purpose, fuelled by productivity, and running happily on the fumes of efficiency. Free time wasn't something I longed for; it was something I avoided. It gave me space to think; thinking usually led to feeling, and feeling… well, that was where things got messy. When I slowed down long enough to notice what was happening inside me, the feelings either felt too much or turned into more of themselves. Sad became sadder. Tired became bone-deep exhaustion. So, I kept moving and doing and pretending that stillness was overrated.

It's taken me years to understand that feelings aren't trying to ruin our day; they're simply trying to be noticed. And when we ignore them, they don't disappear. They wait, patient and persistent, until they find another way to get our attention.

Last Saturday was a textbook example. I'd somehow landed the holy grail of motherhood, an afternoon of silence. The kids were at a sleepover, Neil was at a work function, and I was home, blissfully alone. You'd think I would lean into it, maybe even read a book like a normal grown-up, but instead, I found myself face-to-face with a few familiar demons whispering that I wasn't doing or being enough. I'd have none of that, so I made toast... then I cleaned the toaster... and the cupboard above it... and before I knew it, I was wiping down every surface in sight, because apparently nothing says *I'm processing my emotions* quite like a spotless kitchen.

In the traffic the following day, those same thoughts came to mind, but this time, I had nowhere to go and nothing to do. London traffic has become such a regular part of my life that I've stopped fighting it. I'd love to say I've embraced it, but honestly, that would be delusional. Accepting it is the best I can do. The upside was that I was strangely present, my mind completely blank, a rare and almost suspicious state for any mother juggling the usual family chaos.

One minute I was admiring the colour of the car ahead; the next, bam, anxiety. Out of nowhere. To be clear, I had absolutely nothing to be anxious about, but there it was leaning in like an uninvited guest asking, "Miss me?"

Every single thought, feeling, or emotion is a signal. When you ignore them, they start knocking louder.

I don't know about you, but I don't exactly open the door and say, "Oh... hi, Anxiety. You're back. Great! Make yourself at home." Or "Guilt! What a surprise. Come in, I was just enjoying a rare moment of peace." They always burst through with energy, ready to unpack their emotional luggage all over my clean floor. Filing them away feels easier. That's why women like me stay glued to the hamster wheel of life. Cleaning the toaster, the plug point, and the cupboard above it feels far safer than sitting still. *Stick to the status quo* might as well be my motto.

On one hand, it worked. I was getting things done. There's satisfaction in that, a little internal pat on the back that says, *Look at you, productive queen.* But I wasn't addressing what was going on inside me.

Isn't that what wine and sleep are for? Why did it go deeper when the surface is holding? Fair questions. I used to ask them too.

It took me a while to realise there was nothing mysterious about it. Our brains are wired to focus on what's wrong. It's called "negativity bias," basically the leftover setting from when "what's wrong" might have teeth. Back then, it kept us alive; now it just keeps mothers twitchy. We're constantly scanning for the next crisis, listening for the crash, anticipating the chaos, noticing when our child isn't thriving, and when we're not enough, so if I was sitting quietly in traffic, you can be sure an intrusive thought would eventually wander in. It's outdated programming, and honestly, I'd quite like an upgrade.

If we don't intentionally notice and name what's happening inside, those unprocessed thoughts and feelings stack up quietly until one day they burst out during a minor domestic crisis, like someone loading the dishwasher *wrong*.

We can't change the wiring, but we can work with it. Pausing long enough to notice and name what we feel creates clarity and space for emotions like gratitude, contentment, and peace—feelings that rarely get a look when our minds are cluttered with unprocessed noise.

I share this because, while this book is about emotions and helping our children make sense of theirs, the work starts with *us*. Mothers are brilliant at keeping everything afloat, but checking in with our own emotions rarely makes the list.

Since training as a life coach, I've had to do a lot of work on myself. It sounds admirable, but the truth is, you can't guide anyone else through their feelings if you're unwilling to face your own. When it comes to our children, that truth runs even deeper. We lay the foundation for their emotional growth, and that begins with our own awareness.

So, let's rewind to the quiet house, the one blissfully free of "Maaaarm" echoing down the passage. On that day, I did something uncharacteristic and sank into the sofa for a bit of daytime TV. What a luxury to choose something myself and not have to wrestle the remote from the sport-obsessed testosterone in my house. I could have framed the moment.

Scrolling past cookery shows and property makeovers, I stopped at a psychological drama about four mothers juggling life. On the surface, they looked composed, yet beneath it all was a familiar mix of guilt, overwhelm, and quiet ache, feelings carefully tucked away from the world. Maybe it was because they looked like someone I might bump into at school pick-up; maybe it was the exhaustion in their eyes, but as I watched, I realised I wasn't just seeing their story unfold; I was seeing a version of my own.

I'd become an expert at smiling through gritted teeth, at performing *everything's fine* with Oscar-worthy conviction while my thoughts and feelings stacked precariously inside. Who needs therapy when you've got primetime television holding up a mirror? It gave me a real laugh until I realised that I wasn't just seeing myself on screen; I was being called out by it.

What I'd been calling "normal stress" was actually something deeper. The more I ignored it, the louder it got. It started sneaking out in the usual ways: I'd snap over unfinished homework, sigh too loudly when a child took too long to exit the car, or feel personally attacked by the mess in the house. It was never really about those things, but in the moment, I couldn't see.

Really, it was about being out of sync with myself. The part of my brain that's supposed to fix everything clocked off early and left the emotional department pressing all the buttons at once. I kept thinking I needed a better system or a new routine, but what I really needed was the nerve to look underneath it all—to do the work beneath the work of motherhood.

The turning point in the TV series showed how years of not paying attention, of swallowing emotions, and simply pushing through can ripple outwards, touching partners, children, friends, and even neighbours.

Come on, Leonora, it's only a TV show. Fair enough. But it made me think about the quieter consequences in my own life, and the ways my unspoken feelings shaped my family. Some of the damage was subtle, hidden in sighs and silences, but some stretched across whole seasons.

You see, I'd lost touch with a bit of myself, and without noticing, I started reacting instead of responding, bracing instead of feeling. It left me tired in a way sleep couldn't fix and short-tempered in ways that didn't match the mother I thought I was. I had to learn to notice and name what I felt so I could find my way back to myself.

Interestingly, the moment that helped me see this didn't come from my mid-morning act of defiance on the sofa. It came from Neil, my husband of nearly thirty years, who, in the most ordinary way, managed to say out loud what I had been trying to figure out for years.

It was a Saturday morning. I was standing at the kitchen counter eating breakfast when he wandered in, wearing Crocs and boxer shorts. It's not a look I love, which made his opening line all the more unexpected.

"I didn't realise I still turned heads," he said, completely straight-faced.

I wasn't sure whether to laugh or call for medical attention.

"Sorry, what?" I asked, mid-chew.

He went on to explain that the day before, he'd attended a women's conference at his office and had volunteered to share some of his views.

His views? This is going to be interesting, I thought.

He paused for a moment, then said, "After watching your growth over the past few years, I've come to realise we got something wrong. When you became a mother, the focus should have stayed on you, your well-being, your development, and your emotional health. We should have protected that and tried to better understand you. If we had, everything else would have felt a little lighter."

His words landed like a truth I'd known but hadn't dared to claim. Being a mother may be central to who you are, but it's not the whole of you. The parts that exist beyond that role deserve as much care.

You're not here to perfect motherhood, but to live it, finding meaning in the chaos and holding both joy and mess without pretending one cancels the other. At the heart is paying attention to what's happening inside, giving your feelings room to breathe, and finding the words to name them. Emotional awareness isn't just something to pass on to your children. It's something you need to practise for yourself. Not because it's trendy, but because it reminds you that what you feel matters.

So, before I take you into the tools and insights, I want to start with the version of me who didn't know any of this and the effects this had on my relationship with my children. That's where the real story begins.

THE IDENTITY LEAK

Meet me ...

Before I had children, my life ran on structure. I worked in the corporate world, where efficiency and organisation were second nature. I loved a good system, a neatly crossed-off list, and the satisfaction of meeting a goal ahead of schedule. Confidence came easily when success could be measured by deadlines met and reports completed. I was driven, focused, and quietly proud of being the person everyone could count on to get things done.

When I stepped away from that world to raise my children, I didn't really change gears. I simply transferred them. I brought the same discipline, standards, and instinct to achieve. Only this time, the project wasn't coordinating trainee intakes or planning client events. It was motherhood, and I approached it with the quiet determination that had once helped me bring order to spreadsheets and schedules, not yet realising that this new role would ask something entirely different.

At the time, I was living in London, and I still remember the thrill of handing in my notice. No more long commutes, office politics, or dull interview sessions where I had to ask every potential trainee the same tired questions. What I saw ahead was a slower pace, a bit of freedom, and maybe even the chance to explore my creative side, as if motherhood were a kind of sabbatical where I'd finally discover myself through finger-painting and home-baked muffins.

The thought makes me laugh now. Long commutes? Try driving the same school route for decades. Mundane? Yes, very. And the politics? Let's not dress it up. Sibling rivalry, plain and simple. "Mom, why did he get more than me?" "Can I sit in the front, because she did last time?" Even now, with three grown children, I still get the occasional, "Who's your favourite?" Internal politics, indeed.

Having said that, I enjoyed the transition into motherhood. One became two, and a few years later, I was blessed with a third. I taught them our beliefs and values, kept track of lost socks, and organised my Tupperware like my sanity depended on it. I found it quite incredible how you can spend years studying, climbing ladders, and collecting qualifications, only to end up sitting cross-legged on a bathroom floor, cheering on a toddler for producing what can only be described as a teaspoon of dribble. For raisins. Actual raisins. And when they do, there are high-fives, victory texts, and maybe even a commemorative photo of the potty (don't pretend you haven't thought about it). Who needs career milestones when you've got bodily-function success stories? Motherhood really is the strangest promotion I've ever had, and I absolutely loved it.

There were a few minor hiccups (like losing a child on Oxford Street during the height of London summer, a stress nobody wants to go through), but apart from that, I discovered that I was as good at being a mother as anything I'd done before. All my corporate superpowers—the attention to detail, high standards, and an almost competitive commitment to ticking things off—transferred beautifully into family life. I called it structure or routine, but really, it was control. Plain and simple.

That's where I began to get stuck.

If everything looked perfect on the outside, I didn't have to face what was happening on the inside. For a while, that worked, but thoughts and feelings, whatever you want to call them, need somewhere to go. Looking back, I can see that what I was really creating wasn't calm or control but a world so tightly managed that there was no room left for me. Which probably explains why, with an embarrassing level of pride, I routinely sorted the LEGO by colour. I know. Who does that? Especially when the kids immediately upend the boxes and stir the whole thing like soup?

And yet, appearances mattered. I carried a bag that was part Mary Poppins, part mobile triage unit, and it suited me perfectly. Inside you'd find wipes, plasters, hand sanitiser, spare pants (not mine), a rogue dinosaur, and always a chocolate bar for moments when bribery felt like the only way forward. If you rummaged deep enough, you could probably have stocked a small branch of Boots.

[An aside, just the other day, as we sat in church, my twenty-three-year-old leaned over, half joking, and whispered, "Mom, do you have a snack?" To his amazement, I did. I reached into my trusty bag and produced one, as if it were the most natural thing in the world. Some habits die hard.]

I wore that efficiency like a party trick. People noticed. Friends, teachers, even the bin man once gave me a respectful nod for my perfectly labelled recycling bins. "You're so organised," they'd say. "You make it look easy." And with every comment, I'd give my invisible Supermom badge a discreet polish, because making motherhood look seamless, at least from the outside, felt important.

Inside told a very different story. I thought I was figuring it out, collecting advice, building systems, and keeping everything under control, when really, what I needed was to turn some of that energy inward and start understanding myself, not just managing everything around me.

Don't get me wrong: there was more to motherhood than my obsession with order. I loved the closeness of it and the everyday intimacy of being central to someone's world. Yet, the more I became "Mom," the more the rest of me disappeared into the background. I didn't question it because I was too busy perfecting the performance of keeping everyone else happy. Every flicker of my discomfort was neatly filed in my favourite mental folder, labelled "Deal with Later." (You will notice a trend.)

Over the years, that mental file grew steadily heavier. Inner discomfort has a sneaky way of showing up in different disguises. For some, it's buried so deep you almost forget it exists; for others, it hovers closer to the surface, tugging for attention while you get better at pretending not to notice. I fell firmly into that second group. The silence often felt too loud, and I'd ache for conversation that didn't involve sleep schedules or remedies for sore gums. I'd remind myself how lucky I was to be home and how many women would trade places in a heartbeat, but the gratitude always tangled with guilt, because loneliness wasn't something mothers were supposed to confess.

There was also the quiet sting of being left behind—watching old colleagues climb ladders while I was stuck building towers out of Duplo, shrinking a little each time someone asked what I did. "I'm just at home with the kids," I'd say, and the word "just" carried more weight than I liked to admit.

The truth was, I missed me. I missed being seen as someone who wasn't defined only by how useful I was to my family. Don't get me wrong. I loved those tea parties with a one-eyed bear and a doll covered in hand-drawn tattoos, but even in their sweetness, a small part of me ached for the woman who used to know who she was. And because I didn't know how to say that, I packed those feelings away and focused on what I could control. That was strength, pushed to perfection.

If I could keep the systems tight, the chaos managed, and everyone in check, then maybe I wouldn't have to face the uncertainty rising inside me. So, I pressed on, determined to have the neatest home, the most balanced meal plan, and a family chore chart that others might admire. My kids were in bed by seven, their hair brushed, their teeth clean, and their prayers whispered as thanks rather than full-blown negotiations. It was polished parenting at its finest, or so I liked to think.

My little truth tellers started calling me Captain von Trapp, after the strict father in *The Sound of Music*. Same tone, without the whistle or the singing nuns. Like him, I'd misplaced the softer parts of myself. They got the efficient mother, the one who barked orders and marched through the day. The fun, relaxed version of me made only brief appearances, usually when guests were over or when I was performing the role of the effortlessly warm mom. Classic signs of a woman with too much locked inside.

But order never lasts. Thoughts, feelings, purpose—all the things we push aside, wait. And they don't always wait patiently. Take a certain birthday party for one of my children, for example...

I couldn't even tell you which child's birthday it was, because let's face it, after a while, they do blur together. All I know is that there was a haze of balloons taped to every surface and sugar-high children bouncing off the walls, or in this case, a bouncy castle that had given up and was sagging like it needed a nap. Given that I was still icing a pirate ship cake at one in the morning, I was pretty shattered, but I pressed on, muttering to myself about how the mast wasn't straight. It had so many skewers holding it together that it could have doubled as a medieval weapon, but in my head, it had to resemble cake perfection, and it did. I'd go as far as to say it was fit for the set of *Pirates of the Caribbean* while also being a sponge metaphor of me: propped up, overworked, and held together with whatever I could find.

At the time, I put my crankiness down to party stress. Someone asked where the serviettes were, and I clenched my jaw like I'd just failed a hosting exam. Two boys arrived dressed as Batman. Batman—at a pirate party? I mean, come on. Then Neil, oblivious to it all, sliced the cake the "wrong" way. I snapped. Yes, yes, I know. It was only cake. But it wasn't only cake; it was years of trying to hold it all together and years of swallowing everything I felt, all packed into one overly ambitious sponge ship. But I didn't see that.

Instead, I chose my usual approach, the "smile and wave" routine, perfected by the penguins of *Madagascar*. It had worked for years. Only this time, the feelings were bubbling too close to the surface, and bolting felt like the safer choice. So, I took the only escape route available and hid in the bathroom like it was a bunker. There I sat, on the edge of the bath, staring at the tiles as though they might offer a solution. *I don't even know what I'm feeling*, I thought. *I just know it's too much.*

That moment didn't look like a crisis. The bouncy castle hadn't deflated and swallowed a child whole. No one had slipped peanuts to the one kid who could go into anaphylactic shock just by looking at them. It was far quieter than that, like a slow leak you don't notice until the floor is already wet. By the time I finally did, mine wasn't just damp; it was completely saturated. Years of little leaks long ignored had soaked in so deeply that I couldn't even tell where the first crack had started.

I didn't walk out of that bathroom with a grand epiphany. It was more of a whisper: *You can't keep living like this.* And hidden inside that whisper was an invitation to start paying attention.

It took me a long time to understand that attention doesn't arrive with fanfare. Sometimes it's just sitting still long enough to admit you're lonely, or that you miss being seen as someone other than useful. Sometimes it's allowing yourself to say that motherhood, as sacred and beautiful as it is, can also be dull, repetitive, and achingly isolating. Saying that doesn't make you ungrateful; it makes you human.

If I'd known how to meet myself with that kind of compassion sooner, I think I would have grown differently, and my children would have too. I used to think they were too young to see beyond the surface, but they were taking it all in. Children notice more than we realise, not just how we pack their lunches or celebrate their birthdays, but how we treat ourselves in the middle of it all. They watch whether we honour what we need or quietly push it aside.

What they learned from me was a lesson I never meant to teach: that our needs don't matter, and that if everything looks neat on the surface, no one needs to ask what's going on underneath. That's not the message I want to pass on.

The message we should be passing on to our children is that their worth has nothing to do with how well they cope or how much they achieve. It has everything to do with being fully, humanly themselves. And the only way they'll learn that is if we show them, by paying attention to the quiet voice that says, *Something here needs attention.* Because ignoring that voice always costs more than listening to it.

That's where we'll go next, to the place where all those unprocessed feelings end up, the one labelled, yes, "Deal with Later."

THE COST OF NOT NOTICING

Let's be honest, we mothers know more than we let on. We know that feelings never really go away; they loiter under the bonnet of motherhood, waiting for that sacred moment when the house finally stops vibrating with noise, and then, *bang*, they roar to life like an engine that's been quietly idling for years.

Wouldn't it be nice to be given a service manual—a moment to pull over, check the oil, maybe have a cry on the hard shoulder before merging back onto the motorway of family life? But no. Permission slips still go missing five minutes before they're due. The three a.m. wake-ups still happen, sometimes for nightmares, sometimes for water, and once, in our house, for a full-scale spider evacuation that had to be handled with whispered apologies and ridiculous levels of calm. At three in the morning. Naturally.

For years, I told myself I'd get to me when things settled: when the kids slept better, when school started, and when the house stopped looking like a lost property office. But *when* is a slippery thing. It moves the goalposts every time you get close. Unless I made space on purpose, my own well-being would quietly slide to the bottom of the list, somewhere beneath "find missing PE kit" and "pretend to enjoy PTA bake sales."

The first real crack showed up at the pirate party. From the outside, it looked like any other Saturday afternoon with too much sugar, not enough patience, and a faint smell of Capri Sun in the air. Inside, though, a small voice whispered, *Are you okay?* And I had absolutely no idea how to answer it. So, I did what any self-respecting woman held together by caffeine and wet wipes would do: I smiled and called it strength.

We all do it, don't we? Just ask the version of me who turned up to sports day less than a week after giving birth. There I was, standing in the blazing heat, one child bouncing through the sack race, another plotting an ice-cream ant farm, and a newborn strapped to my chest, insisting on feeding the moment the start whistle blew.

Strength like that can be deceiving. When you're wired to push through, you rarely stop to ask if you should. The truth is, the cracks were already there, seeping into every corner of my life. My patience had worn paper-thin, my fuse was short, and I found myself reacting more than connecting. It didn't take much to tip me over the edge. Sometimes it was a grumpy driver. Other times, it was the classic male betrayal of the toilet seat left up, which left me sitting on freezing porcelain during a midnight wee. Even the calmest among us would have flapped, and flap I did, with enough theatrical flair to make sure the entire house was aware of my suffering. I was clearly unravelling; I just didn't call it that. I called it a "busy season," which would've been fine if it hadn't been my fifteenth in a row.

The slow erosion left me feeling like a stranger to myself. That's when I'd retreat into what I started calling my hidey hole. It wasn't an actual hole, mind you, but something akin to a mental crawl space where I'd disappear when pissed off with the world. In that place, there was no need to be "on." I could linger around the edges of family life like a friendly ghost, nodding at conversations, handing out the odd snack, and occasionally throwing in, "Why don't you make a card for Granny?" before retreating again. It was peaceful in a detached sort of way, like watching my own family on mute.

Emotional withdrawal like that doesn't look broken. It passes for calm, but really, it's disconnection in disguise, and I'm not going to pretend otherwise. When I think about it now, I can see how cluttered my inner world was, but I chose to organise everything else instead. If I couldn't make sense of my feelings, at least I could make sense of the spices. Yes, we're back to my obsession with the spice rack. I maintain it was a legitimate hobby, just in case you're wondering.

My poor family didn't quite know what to make of my hidey hole. It meant that Mom, the central and most present person in our home (and yes, I'm speaking about her in the third person because that's who I used to be), would respond to a question like "What's for dinner?" with

"You guys decide." Not a normal kind of mother response. "Where should we go this weekend, Mom?" "Up to you." "Should we defrost the chicken?" "Don't ask me, I'm in witness protection." You have to love the attempt at the *I'm here but not really* approach to motherhood.

I pretended that's how I'd always been, but my family noticed the difference. And rightly so. Imagine if Donald Trump suddenly decided to sit quietly in a corner and listen. It just doesn't happen. That's how unbelievable my silence was.

You'd think that would have been my moment of clarity, right? The point where I went, *Whoa, hang on, what's going on here, Leonora?* But no. I didn't do that. Instead, I doubled down, pretending to go with the flow and simply give everyone else a turn at the wheel. Instead of saying, "Guys, I need a minute here," I quietly withdrew and behaved as if detachment and agreeableness were perfectly normal. It was ridiculous. But pulling back felt easier than facing what was unsettling me, and I'd become quite skilled at it. But you can't hide from your inner world forever. It always finds a way to make its presence known.

Unfortunately, it took years to begin to understand the cost of not paying attention to myself.

By the time it finally caught up with me, my son Matthew was old enough to wrestle with some big feelings of his own, and for once, instead of diving into my usual "fix-it" mode, I decided to simply listen. As he spoke, something about what he was sharing took me straight back to my early twenties. His emotions mirrored things I'd once felt but never really faced.

Somewhere in that moment, I thought maybe he was old enough to see a bit more of the messy me—the one who doesn't have all the answers. So, I told him about an experience I had years earlier and the emotions that came up as a result. Saying it out loud felt risky, as though I were peeling back a layer I'd carefully hidden. It was heavy with regret, guilt, and the unspoken shame we carry without even realising.

He listened quietly, then said, "That surprises me." When I didn't answer, he added, "It's never occurred to me that you've ever felt things like that."

Of course, he hadn't. Why would he? I had worked so hard to appear "together" that I'd never shown my children what "not together" looked like. If our kids never see us being human, how will they ever believe it's okay to be human themselves?

There was another moment, not quite as serious but equally revealing. We were sitting around the dinner table one evening. It was the kind of ordinary night that doesn't announce itself as significant. There were empty plates, half-drunk mugs of coffee, and the usual noise of family life. Out of nowhere, Matthew turned to his fiancée. He said, with absolute sincerity, "Mom's kind of the base standard for tidiness." I nearly choked. To him, it was a compliment. To me, it was horrifying. What I heard, and what dear Abi heard, was that I've modelled perfection so convincingly that no one else stands a chance.

I laughed, that weird, slightly manic laugh you do when you can't tell if you're joking or crying. Then I said something that made everyone at the table go quiet. "I'm not the base standard of anything," I told them. "The neatness, the structure, and the lists weren't strength. They were a cover-up." They just stared. I went on anyway, because why stop mid-revelation? I told them that behind my chore charts and matching Tupperware was a woman who'd spent years wrestling with fear, anxiety, and regret, all while pretending to be fine. I said I'd convinced myself that if I held everything together, I could somehow control everything around me, but control wasn't safety. It was a brilliant strategy for building emotional Fort Knox. Nobody gets in, nobody gets out, and the only person trapped inside is you.

Many of us don't realise that high standards and quiet pressure can send a burdensome message: *If you're not meeting this invisible baseline, you're not enough.* It's subtle, but it still lands. That's the quiet cost of not noticing.

It's not about standards. It's about being human, and that can only happen when you drop the act and let yourself be seen, flaws and all. The flawed version is the one people connect with, which is ironic, considering I spent years trying to hide those imperfections... and now I'm broadcasting them in a book.

Speaking of which, not noticing showed up for me in how I was...

Using busyness as an attempt to organise my inner world.

Doing gave me structure when everything inside felt messy or uncertain. It was easier to chase the relief of ticking boxes than to sit with discontentment, fear, or anxiety. Given the choice, I'd take feel-good busyness over unsettling stillness any day. The cost, of course, was that the feelings lingered. They waited for quieter moments to slip out sideways: snapping at the kids, sighing over the dinner dishes, or retreating into silence when what I really needed was connection. Busyness gave me temporary relief, but it never gave me peace.

Treating emotion as an interruption.

To me, feelings weren't just uncomfortable; they were inefficient. They slowed me down, pulled me off track, and threatened the smooth running of the day. Who has time to sit and reflect when someone needs a lift to practice, another is shouting for help with maths, and dinner is burning in the oven? They interrupt the flow. I lived as if emotions were an obstacle course to push through rather than signals worth paying attention to.

Modelling composure instead of emotional safety.

I believed being steady meant holding everything in, so they didn't have to worry. What I didn't realise was that I was teaching them that feelings were something to hide. They learnt to bring me their achievements and happy moments in their day, but not always their disappointments, fears, or tears. In trying to protect them from my struggles, I made it harder for them to feel safe with their own.

Losing the language for what mattered.

When someone asked how I was, I'd say "fine" or "busy." They were safe, socially acceptable answers, but they left no room for the truth. Over time, the gap between how I felt and how I functioned widened, and my children noticed. When asked how they were, their reply was a swift and predictable, "I'm fine." They gave back what I had modelled. The cost of that was harder to see at first, but it was there. "I'm fine" became a family script, and it told me more than I wanted to admit.

The truth is, not noticing doesn't always come with big breakdowns or dramatic turning points. Most of the time, it slips quietly into the everyday moments where you stop paying attention to yourself without even realising. From the outside, it looks fine, but beneath the surface, it's a slow drift away from who you are.

If only we were afforded a "do over." It's not about regret. It's about understanding; it's about learning to hold our own story with the same kindness we try to offer everyone else.

And that's exactly where we're heading next.

IF I COULD DO IT OVER

If do-overs were an option, I would have started by hiring someone else to do the organising. And I'm fairly sure I'd have begun with the LEGO, since those tiny plastic bricks seemed to hold up my entire sense of stability. And I'd have thrown in the spice rack too; it was ridiculous how quickly I convinced myself I was thriving just because my cumin and coriander were in straight lines.

Initially, I thought my problems could be solved by finding more time or creating a better routine, as if self-awareness could be scheduled between dinner and bedtime. But it wasn't about time at all. It was about attention—the kind we offer everyone else so freely but rarely give to ourselves. I see it now, especially when I work with other mothers and we talk about connection, not as something we do for others, but as something that begins with us.

A few years ago, I was running a workshop and asked a simple question: "What makes someone a really good friend?" It was an easy one. Everyone had something to share. Kindness, humour, honesty, presence. The list grew quickly. Then I asked, "How many of those things are you offering to yourself?"

That's when the energy in the room shifted. Only moments before, it had been buzzing with laughter and warmth. Now it was quiet. One or two gave that small, nervous laugh we all do when something hits too close to home, but beyond that, silence. Not one of them could say they offered themselves the same kindness or honesty they so freely gave to others. These women weren't broken; they had just become so used to tuning into everyone else that they'd forgotten how to tune into themselves. And I get it because I've done the same. I often wonder how many of us have quietly absorbed the idea that hiding what we feel is the same as handling it. Guess what? It's not.

If I had the chance to do it over, I'd step back from "mom mode" and notice the blur between mother and woman—the role swallowed the person, and the emotions that might have grounded me got buried instead.

In hindsight, I'd ask myself some fundamental questions: *How kind am I being to myself? How honest? How present? How much time am I giving to my own needs?* I'd stop trying to look so cheerfully competent while doing it all. My kids didn't need a polished director keeping the whole show on track. They needed me, just me, in all my messy, uncertain humanness.

I remember one of my sons once saying, "Mom, you always know what to do." At the time, I took it as praise. Now I hear it differently. What he couldn't see was the woman who sometimes didn't have a clue and was scared to admit it. Imagine the freedom in being able to say, "I don't know. This is my first time too. Let's figure it out together." That's presence. Not perfect, just human. And that's the version of me I wish I'd let them see sooner.

If I could do it over, there's so much I'd change. Not because I failed, but because I finally get it. Connection doesn't come from having all the answers; it comes from showing up, wobbly bits and all. If I ever had a chance to rewrite those years, I'd start small. Tiny shifts. The sort of things that seem insignificant at the time but quietly change everything.

If I could do it over, I would...

Share more of me.

Instead of always starting with, "How was your day?" or "What did you do at school?" I wish I'd offered something of myself first. Even a small admission, such as "I'm figuring this out too," would have opened the door to connect in a way questions alone never could. Letting them see the parts of me outside of "Mom" would have painted a fuller picture of who I am and how I process my feelings.

These days, it comes more naturally. If I'm working something through, I'll often say, "I'm not sure what I think yet, so I'm going to talk it out as I go." It's a little messy, but it's real, and more importantly, it shows my family that it's okay to be a work in progress.

Practise emotional agility.

If I could do it over, I would have learned emotional agility so much earlier. Not the polished, clinical kind, but the everyday version, the kind where you can notice feeling without being completely hijacked by them. That tiny gap between feeling something and reacting to it is where your whole life softens.

Back then, I didn't have that gap. I was hooked by whatever emotion showed up first—frustration, fear, guilt—and I let them run the show. I reacted before I even knew I was reacting. If I'd understood emotional agility sooner, maybe I'd have been less snappy over spilt milk, less silent when I needed support, and less obsessed with lists that made me feel capable but kept me from myself.

What I know now is that agility doesn't stop you from feeling things; it just stops the feelings from dragging you around by the collar. You still feel everything, but you're not swallowed whole by it. And if I'd had that back then, I think I would have met myself and my children with a lot more kindness.

Name what's hard.

There's so much I wish I'd known about the power of naming what I was feeling instead of swallowing it down. Silence turned those feelings into clutter that settled quietly inside me, and from there, it began to shape how I saw myself. Over time, what began as "I feel overwhelmed" quietly became "this is just who I am," and that was a much heavier thing to carry.

If I could go back, I would have said it out loud, even in small ways: "This is a lot." "I'm at capacity." "I'm not okay right now." That's simply speaking the truth. There's something about naming a feeling out loud that brings a lightness to it. It's as if the moment breathes again. And it's not just for us, but for everyone around us.

Had I done that more often, I would have shown my kids that you can hold the weight of life without becoming it. They wouldn't have had to second-guess what was going on in my silences, wondering what I was thinking or what I was about to say. They would have seen it as a passing emotion, not a storm to hide from. It would have shown them that feelings aren't dangerous, that they move through us when we let them, and that love is safest when it's honest, not perfect.

What I know now is that we are not our feelings. We are the ones carrying them, and if I'd learned that earlier, I think I would have shown more kindness to them and to myself.

Build myself a bench.

Dr Becky Kennedy, author of *Good Inside*, talks about something she calls the "Feelings Bench." It's a place where you sit beside your child and let them feel what they feel without rushing in to fix it. I wish I'd offered myself that same kindness. A place to sit beside my own feelings and say, *This is hard. I believe you. I'm here.*

No one tells you that when you become a mother, you're still allowed to matter in the story you're writing. You're not just the narrator, guiding everyone else through their plot lines. You're part of the story too. A full character. You have feelings, fears, and needs that deserve to be seen, not only by others but by you.

That's what emotional growth really is. It's remembering that you belong to yourself as much as you belong to your family. Whether your kids are toddlers, teenagers, or towering over you at the fridge, it's never too late to pause, notice, and begin again.

So, what about you? When was the last time you checked in with yourself—properly? When you spend your days holding everything together, showing up, pushing through, and quietly performing your role with military-level efficiency, do you forget what you need, and eventually, forget you're even allowed to have needs?

In the next chapter, I'll show you what began to shift when I started practising presence with myself. It wasn't only about what I did differently, but what softened when I finally made space for my own emotions to breathe.

FINDING MY WAY BACK

I never pictured myself as someone who'd talk about mindfulness or emotional presence. To me, those words belonged to women with yoga mats tucked under one arm and herbal tea in their hands. Lovely people, I'm sure, but I didn't see myself in their world. And besides, inner work sounded like work, and I already had plenty of that on my plate. What I failed to grasp was that ignoring myself was costing me more than the chaos ever did.

Then the pandemic hit. Overnight, the house filled with nearly grown children—one camped at the dining table doing A-levels, another back from university, and the youngest rolling his eyes at online learning, claiming he had COVID to avoid work (apparently, rest and recovery involved a lot of Xbox and pizza).

This was supposed to be my *when* season: *When* they're older ... *when* things settle ... *when* I finally get to focus on me. But *when* has a way of disappearing, leaving the other me, the one tucked beneath *Mom me*, waiting her turn.

Out of sheer desperation, I signed up for some life coaching, led by someone clever enough to get ahead of the pandemic's online boom. I had no idea what I was getting into, only that if I didn't try something, I'd stay stuck. I was hoping for a quick fix, a motivational quote, maybe even a plan. What I'd really been handed was an uncomfortable amount of time to sit with myself.

I think that's what happened to so many of us during the pandemic. The noise stopped, the distractions vanished, and suddenly we were face to face with our own lives. No more running, no more hiding behind busy. Just us, and the feelings we'd spent years neatly boxing up. Time isn't what keeps us from living; it's what's been quietly inviting us back all along. We just have to stop waiting for it to arrive all polished and peaceful. It never does. We build it, fiercely and imperfectly, or life will build it for us in ways we didn't choose.

Having that space and then being intentional about how I used it was unfamiliar territory. I've always liked the phrase "me, myself, and I." It sounds light-hearted, but when you think about it, there is a beauty in holding all that space. No distractions, no roles to play, and no one else to hide behind. It was in that quiet that I came across a word I'd never really contemplated before: self-awareness. I knew it, but I'd never understood its true meaning.

Self-awareness is the practice of noticing yourself without judgment and learning to see what's going on inside before it spills out sideways. For some, this comes easily. They dive right in. For others, it's awkward, confronting, even a little lonely. But it's also one of the kindest things you can ever do for yourself.

At first, I saw it simplistically. *I'm tired, cranky, and I've had too much coffee.* That's awareness, but the deeper kind is far more honest. It doesn't just ask the question: *What's going on with me?* It stays still long enough to actually hear the answer.

Tired isn't always just tired. Sometimes it means, *Go to bed, woman.* Sometimes it means, *Stop pretending that scrolling Instagram at midnight counts as winding down.* Other times, it's your body saying, *Move me. I've been sitting still for two days, and I'm starting to fuse with the chair.* It's the same feeling, but with very different instructions. How on earth will you know which one it is if you never stop to ask?

That's what this whole self-awareness thing boils down to. It's giving meaning to what you're feeling instead of brushing it off. Once you start connecting those dots, your choices begin to shift. Even your compassion grows, because you're not just reacting anymore; you're paying attention. And, of course, once I started noticing all this, I brought my usual tendencies with me.

As a perfectionist, I wanted to get everything right, even the business of self-awareness. This new concept of navel-gazing quickly became another way to spot all the ways I was failing. I treated it like a performance review for my emotions, ticking off where I could've done better. Only now do I see it's the complete opposite. Self-awareness is about listening. It's the gentle pause where you notice what's happening inside and offer kindness instead of criticism. The real growth isn't in what you do next; it's in finally understanding yourself without needing to tidy anything up.

Of course, knowing that and *doing* it are two different things. I had to start somewhere, and the simplest place was right where I already was.

Do you brush your teeth every day? I hope so, because that's my moment. I've attached self-awareness to something I already do. Since I brush my teeth first thing, it's the perfect time to check in with myself: *How are you feeling this morning? What one small thing would help improve your mood?* Later in the day, if I catch myself snapping, I might think, *Oh, right, your period's late. Time to soften, not push harder.* Some nights, I even do a quick body audit before bed: *How does your body feel right now? What do you need to let go of before sleep?*

These aren't grand rituals or lofty mindfulness goals. They're two-minute check-ins that change the way I meet myself. Self-awareness isn't another thing on the to-do list; it's simply noticing what's already there.

One afternoon, I was standing at the top of the stairs, clutching a laundry basket like it was Exhibit A in the case against motherhood. Inside were trousers still knotted into underwear, socks rolled into cricket balls, and a smell I couldn't quite identify. My emotions were louder than the moment deserved. Truthfully, it wasn't about the laundry. I was tired of being the invisible house fairy, and the basket tipped the balance. In the past, I might've dumped the whole lot across the landing or launched into a full-scale "nobody appreciates me" speech. I've done both, and yes, it's satisfying for about five seconds. This time, I sat down on the top step and asked myself, *Okay, Leonora, what's this really about?*

The answer told me everything I needed to know. I'd had a bad night's sleep, was wrestling with a work task that wouldn't click, it was already five o'clock, and I had no idea what I was making for dinner. Knowing that changed my perspective and what I did next. "Boys, please untangle your clothes before they go in the basket. It makes it easier for everyone." No drama. No explosion. Just honesty. It was such a small moment, but it showed me what's possible when you pause and name what's really going on. That pause creates space between the feeling and the reaction.

It could so easily have gone another way. I could have blurted out my irritation, and they would have come back with the all-too-familiar, "Just chill, Mom," which, as every mother knows, is the single fastest way to lose your cool. But instead, I caught myself.

Over time, these little check-ins became second nature. It wasn't just about a single feeling anymore; it was about the old scripts running in the background. The critic, the fixer, and the controller, my inner committee, who had been running the show for years. Their favourite word was *should*. I should've cooked better, been calmer, done more. No one else needed to judge me; I was doing that just fine. Once I saw them for what they were, they lost their grip. Instead of trying to silence them, I started saying, *Ah, there you are. Thanks for trying to help, but I've got this.*

It sounds simple, but that tiny shift is everything. The moment you name what's happening inside, you stop being run by it. You step out of autopilot and back into yourself. That's what presence really is. Not calm perfection or endless patience, but a quiet knowing of who's in charge.

Seeing those patterns didn't make them disappear, but it gave me the chance to meet myself with compassion, and once I did, that compassion started to spill over. I began to see how often I pointed out what my kids weren't doing instead of celebrating what they were. I'd been living through the lens of "not enough, not right, not quite there," and I'd become so fluent in it that I passed it on without even realising. No wonder everything felt heavy.

This might explain why I once asked Neil for something no mother usually gets: a performance appraisal. I said it with a laugh, because if there's one thing I know how to do, it's make a joke out of a minor breakdown. Beneath the humour, what I really wanted to know was simple: *Am I doing okay? Does this even matter?*

To his credit, he took it seriously. He typed it up on fancy paper, as if he were the CEO of Family Life Inc. It was thoughtful and thorough, outlining achievements and even listing "growth opportunities." It made me laugh, but it also made me cry. He put words to emotions I'd buried, and in hearing them named, I realised how quickly I dismissed my inner world. Maybe, just maybe, if I could learn to honour those feelings myself, something inside me might shift too.

That letter stayed with me, not because of what it said, but because of what it showed me. I'd spent years looking for evidence that I was doing enough, when what I really wanted was permission to feel enough. There's a difference. The first keeps you striving, proving, and collecting gold stars in the form of clean kitchens and functioning children. The second asks you to stop, breathe, and remember that your worth was never something you had to earn.

I wish I'd known sooner that the version of me my family needed wasn't the polished, perfect one. It was the real one. The one who could say, "I don't know," or "that hurt," or even, "I'm doing the best I can."

When we drop the performance, we create space for love, empathy, and emotional safety to grow. Vulnerability isn't about falling apart. It's about being real in a world that constantly tells mothers to be more, do more, and keep it together. Choosing realness is deeply restorative.

Since paying attention to my own needs and emotions, I've rediscovered parts of Leonora I thought I'd lost. When my confidence slipped, awareness nudged me toward rebuilding it. When I felt flat, it showed me I wasn't growing and pushed me toward learning again. When frustration bubbled up, I saw it wasn't about the laundry or the noise; it was about craving stimulation and challenge. Each time, noticing gave me clarity to act.

The hidey hole became a place I owned. There are still times I like to go there. The difference now is that the people closest to me know it exists. If someone says, "You've been quiet," I can reply, "You're right, I'm in my hidey hole." Self-awareness has freed me because now I can name it, communicate it, and ask others to check in before I stay there too long.

That's the quiet power of emotional literacy. It doesn't just soften the hard edges; it brings clarity where there was once confusion. Instead of snapping or retreating, I can pause long enough to recognise what's happening underneath. Maybe I'm tired, maybe I'm stretched thin, or maybe I just need a moment to breathe. From that steadier place, I can show up differently for my kids. They no longer have to play "guess mom's mood." They can relax because I'm more in touch with my whole self and can usually explain what's going on. That steadiness gives them permission to have feelings without fear and to speak up without bracing for impact. We don't always get it right, but over time, it's built a home grounded in trust, where emotions are allowed to exist safely. The gift of this work is that when you find yourself, you bring your children with you.

I wonder who I would've become if I'd kept silencing the woman underneath the "Mom" me. The truth is, she wasn't going anywhere; she was just waiting to be noticed. Once I gave her space, everything shifted: my parenting, my marriage, and my sense of self. Finding my way back was about letting all of me have a seat at the table. From there, connection stopped being something I had to chase. It began to grow naturally, right in the middle of real life.

Now, before you think I'm about to leave you with a little information on self-awareness and the expectation that you will now be nailing it, raising emotionally fluent children, and running a family worthy of a mindfulness documentary, don't worry; I've got you. Real life is still messy, loud, and unpredictable. Toothpaste ends up on mirrors, someone will always need something, and your self-awareness practice might last all of thirty seconds before someone yells, "Mom!" from another room. But I promise, taking a few simple steps toward yourself will end up far better than you ever expected.

What I *am* going to do now is share a few tools that have genuinely helped me and the people I've worked with build more awareness. They're not fancy or time-consuming, and they don't require incense, chanting, or Lycra. Just simple, real-world ways to pause, check in, and come back to yourself before the day carries you away. Think of them as small handholds for when life feels slippery.

TOOLS FOR EMOTIONAL GROWTH

If self-awareness were as simple as asking a few deep questions while brushing your teeth, we'd all be floating through life like emotionally enlightened saints. But that's not how real life works. Real life involves empty fridges, late homework, and losing your phone while you're on it. And yet, these days you can't swing a yoga mat without hitting a mindfulness podcast, a positive parenting post, or an AI-generated guide to emotional regulation. It's all good until it starts to sound like another job.

What I'm offering are a few simple, real-world practices that have helped me, and many others, find a little steadiness in the middle of the chaos.

Tool 1: External Reset ("What's real right now?")

Let's rewind to me, at the top of the stairs, clutching a laundry basket like it contained the meaning of life. I was seconds away from flinging the cricket-ball socks at whoever had created them. I knew what I was feeling, but my brain wasn't exactly queuing up a helpful alternative. What it *really* wanted to do was sprint straight to the worst-case scenario.

There have been so many moments like that, where I've gone from A to B in under ten seconds.

A: A basket of socks so tightly tangled I'd need pliers to separate them.

B: If they can't untangle their socks now, how will they ever survive adulthood?

And there it is, the leap from laundry to life failure. Impressive, really. One moment, it's socks; the next, you're picturing them living in a flat surrounded by takeaway boxes because you never taught them how to pair socks.

That's why we need an out. A mental Ctrl+Alt+Delete before the spiral kicks in and drags the whole family down with it.

It's as simple as a single question: "What's happening right now?" Not next week or when they're twenty-five and can't get a job because they left their trousers inside their pants. Just this moment.

For example:

1. What am I feeling? Am I frustrated, irritated, a little weary of doing so much without acknowledgement?

2. What's going on here? Is it about me, or is it about the kids? Where does the actual issue lie?

3. What are my choices? Do I explode, or ask for help, calmly, humanly?

These questions are tools that help with the bigger picture. Maybe your child just failed a spelling test or lost an important football match. Raging on about socks in the laundry basket won't be the best way to settle his emotions or yours. "What's happening?" gives you a glimpse of the whole scene before you jump into it. It gives you that tiny bit of breathing room between the feeling and the fallout. You don't need to book a retreat or sit in silence for three days. All that's required is a little practice. "What's happening right now?" can take you from sock fury to something that resembles composure.

And here's the reset. "Boys, please remove your pants from your trousers before putting them in the laundry, and it would be easier if you untangle your socks. They'd wash better, too."

Simple. Clear. Everyone's a winner.

I don't usually turn to elite athletes for wisdom on motherhood, but occasionally someone throws in a line that sticks. Novak Djokovic, better known for his killer serve than his emotional regulation, once said, "You can't be present all the time. We're human, and our minds wander." That's the kind of realism I can get behind, because let's be honest, there will be days when you do fling the socks down the stairs.

There will be moments when your teen is mid-rant about curfews, or your toddler has climbed out of his cot for the umpteenth time. You won't find me raising my hand like a traffic officer saying, "Excuse me, I just need a moment to ground myself and locate my inner wisdom." (Actually, I'm going to try it one day, just to see their response.)

This is where Novak's advice comes in handy. You won't get it right all the time, and that's okay. The more you practise presence, the quicker you'll bounce back. Of course, I'm not suggesting you follow a meltdown with tennis drills. What I am saying is that the more you practise noticing, the sooner you recover when life throws you sideways.

That's the quiet power of this reset. Not that you'll never snap, but that you'll catch yourself sooner, soften faster, and find your way back with a little more grace each time.

Tool 2: Internal Reset ("How am I, really?")

In his book *Man's Search for Meaning*, Viktor Frankl writes: "Between the stimulus and response there is a space. In that space is our power to choose our response, and in our response lies our growth and freedom." It's a beautiful truth, but that "space" often feels about the size of a pinhead.

When my youngest was four, socks were his nemesis. Without fail, the pair he was trying to put on before school "didn't feel right." Not Monday's socks. Not Wednesday's. I tried changing their colours, and that didn't even work. While he wrestled with the betrayal of poorly stitched seams, I was trying to get all of us out the door for two different school drop-offs. What was building in me wasn't only stress. It was the quiet emotional storm made up of too many mornings like this one: frustration, resentment, overwhelm, and, underneath it all, the guilt of how angry I often felt before the day had even begun. Whatever space existed between stimulus and response felt completely out of reach.

If I could go back and offer that younger version of me one pearl of wisdom, it would be that some moments aren't meant to be fixed. They simply are what they are, and the best we can do is move through them, carrying a little Djokovic-style bounce-back.

There will be other, less infuriating moments, when a simple check-in isn't only possible, it's powerful. The more we practise those small pauses in calmer moments, the more naturally they show up when we need them most.

That's where the emotional check-in comes in. A few questions you might ask yourself:

1. How did I sleep last night? (This alone explains a *lot*.)

2. Have I eaten anything nourishing today?

3. Is something or someone taking up more mental space than I realised?

4. What might tip the scales today?

5. Am I holding something in that I haven't said out loud?

6. Do I need support, or just five quiet minutes to regroup?

Think of it as your emotional weather report. You don't control the forecast, but knowing whether it's sunny or stormy changes how you step outside.

Just between us, this is one of those rare occasions where I wholeheartedly encourage cheating. The kind I'm endorsing is the Post-it version. Write the questions down, scribble them on the back of a receipt, pin them to your fridge, or tuck them into your car's sun visor. When your mind's already overloaded by sock seams, you don't need to be digging through memory files. Let the cheat sheet do the remembering for you.

When there's more room, you can go deeper:

1. What's really bothering me right now?
2. Am I reacting to this moment, or dragging in three others from the week?
3. What do I wish someone would give me right now, and is there a way I can give it to myself?

You won't always have answers, but even asking the questions is like opening a window. Sometimes, that's all you need.

Tool 3: Mental Push-Ups That Don't Require Lycra

There came a point when I realised understanding my emotions wasn't enough; I needed to retrain my brain. Enter the work of Shirzad Chamine, author of *Positive Intelligence*. His message stopped me in my tracks. He gave language to things I'd only begun to notice.

He introduced me to something he calls "PQ reps"— and I call tiny resets for a busy mother's brain. Just like a muscle grows with small reps in the gym, your brain strengthens when you practise bringing attention to your senses. These micro-moments interrupt the mental spin and bring you back into the here and now, where you can reset and ask the questions we explored earlier.

Here are two I use all the time:

Fingertip Focus

- Rub your fingertips together slowly, noticing the tiny ridges and texture of your skin. It sounds odd, I know, but it's strangely calming. I do it while pretending to scroll my phone in the car park, so I don't look like a woman doing mindfulness in public. Within seconds, my brain gets the memo: calm down, we're fine.

There's science behind it, too. When you focus on touch, you activate the cortex, the part of your brain linked to physical sensation. This gentle shift draws activity away from the amygdala, which is responsible for stress and threat detection. In other words, by tuning into something as simple as your fingertips, you're literally rewiring your brain to feel more grounded. It's mindfulness in its most discreet form, no incense, Lycra, or mountain retreat required.

Three-Breath Reset

- Take three slow breaths. In through your nose, out through your mouth. Notice the air, cool in, warm out. Rest your hand on your stomach and feel it rise and fall. It tells your body, *You're safe,* and dials down the stress response.

Here, you are activating the vagus nerve, which is part of your body's natural "rest and restore" mode. It lowers your heart rate, calms your mind, and tells your nervous system that you're not in danger, even when every time you ask your teen to help clear the table, they mysteriously disappear to the loo. Just three breaths can shift you from frazzled to functional, and the best part is, no one even has to know you're doing it.

These are small things, I know. But they make a difference. Fingertip focus helps bring you back into your body, and breath softens the edges of the moment. I find this especially helpful in those times when what I really need is kindness and compassion. It's a moment to whisper with each inhale, "You've got this, Leonora. You're doing a great job."

The pre-coaching version of me would've rolled her eyes at this and muttered something about not having time for fingertip rubbing or deep breathing, but even the tiniest pause can trigger a shift in your brain. It lights up the parts associated with empathy, calm, and creativity, while quieting the parts that fuel overthinking and the inner critic. In other words, it gives your brain a chance to work with you rather than against you.

Do my kids tease me about it? Absolutely. "Shhh... Mom's doing her weird fingertip thing again." I smile knowing that they're storing it away, even if they don't realise it yet.

Tool 4: Practising Gratitude

Like most of the things I've shared so far, this one didn't come naturally. The idea that gratitude could shift the way I felt seemed far-fetched. When I first heard it, I thought, *Really? Sounds like something you'd see stitched on a cushion with a pastel sunset.* This journey of being more curious about mindfulness has taught me to stay open, even when something feels cliché, and if you throw in a little science, all the better. The research shows that tiny shifts in attention, repeated over time, can rewire your brain.

You have to pause and marvel at that. The brain is wired to scan for the negative. Fact. But sprinkle in a little gratitude, and things begin to turn around. Gratitude nudges your focus from what's missing to what's already here. Think of it as a nervous system top-up.

It doesn't have to be profound. In fact, the smaller and more specific, the better. Last week mine were:

1. Seeing my garden while I worked from home.
2. My teenager saying more than "I'm fine" when I picked him up.
3. Waking up feeling healthy.

Not earth-shattering. Just real.

So how does this connect to emotional regulation? Gratitude's like a gentle counterweight when emotions start doing the cha-cha. It doesn't cancel the feelings; it just stops them from running the show. It softens frustration, calms the spiral, and buys you a few seconds to decide how you actually want to respond.

Gratitude found its way into our family life on the school run, with my youngest sitting beside me. He was about twelve, and when I first nudged him to give it a go, his reply was, "I'm grateful for being grateful." This wasn't the heart-melting moment I'd imagined, but it was something. So, I kept going, day after day, even when it felt like a one-woman gratitude show.

Months later, we were back in the car. I was quiet, not really myself, and honestly tempted to drop the whole gratitude thing. Then he turned to me and said, "What are you grateful for today, Mom?" I could've cried. He hadn't just remembered; he'd absorbed it and handed it back when I needed it most. Proof that the seeds we plant don't grow on schedule, but they do take root.

Tool 5: The Talking Tool (say it out loud)

If there's one thing I've learned, it's that you can't always think your way to clarity; you have to talk your way there. Not through a moan or a rant (though we all have those), but by letting your thoughts tumble out, half-formed and awkward, until they start to make sense. I often don't know what I really think or feel until I've said it out loud, and even then, the first version's rarely right. So, I try again and again until it lands closer to the truth.

This isn't about dumping on someone or spiralling into "poor me." It's about finding a trusted friend, partner, or coach—someone who helps you give shape to what's sitting heavy inside. When we speak, we slow our thoughts down just enough to catch them, and when someone listens—not to solve but simply to hold space—the tangled bits begin to loosen.

You know that feeling when you've been carrying something around for days, then finally say it out loud and realise it's not as terrifying as it felt? That's the talking tool at work. Sometimes the words that come out aren't even the real issue, but they lead you there. One thread loosens, another follows, and suddenly you can see clearly.

Talking is emotional processing in motion. It's how we metabolise our inner world—not to burden others, but to lighten ourselves. And often, without meaning to, we give the other person permission to do the same. There's something healing about being witnessed in your honesty; it invites honesty in return.

So, if you're sitting with something that won't settle, try saying it out loud. Call a friend who listens without fixing. Take a walk and talk it through with your partner. If all else fails, ask Alexa. Anything that gets the words moving, because once they start to flow, so does the clarity.

These tools are about slowing the spin just enough to notice what's really happening, inside and out. Sometimes that means grounding yourself in the present moment; sometimes it's checking in with your own emotional weather; sometimes it's a ten-second reset with your breath or fingertips; and sometimes it's choosing to notice what's good in the middle of the mess. Small things, yes, but stitched together, they become a quiet kind of strength.

FREQUENTLY ASKED QUESTIONS

By this point, you might have a few questions. You're not alone. These are some of the questions I hear most often, not just from other mothers, but often from that little voice inside myself.

Q1: What if I'm trying to be emotionally present, but I still feel like I'm getting it wrong?

Emotional presence isn't about getting it perfect. It's about being willing to *look, listen,* and *try again.* Some days you'll think, *Yes, I'm finally getting this;* other days you'll think, *What am I even doing?* The fact that you're paying attention, even imperfectly, means you're moving in the right direction.

Q2: If my kids are already older, will working on me impact the way we connect?

Whether your child is three or thirty-three, emotional connection is never off the table. In fact, older kids often surprise you—they notice when something in you softens, when you start showing up with a bit more honesty and less armour. It reminds them that growth isn't a childhood phase; it's lifelong.

And just so we're clear, this work isn't only for them. It's for you too. When you feel a little more grounded, everything else feels a little more doable.

Q3: What if I try these tools and they don't work?

These aren't miracle fixes; they're small habits that build something stronger over time. One gym session won't give you abs (and if it does, please send me your workout). Emotional presence works the same way. It's a muscle, and you're strengthening it. Sometimes it'll work, and sometimes it won't. That doesn't mean you've failed; it means you're learning.

Q4: Does this mean I can never lose my temper again?

If only. You're still human, and humans snap sometimes. What matters is what happens next. Do you name it, own it, and repair it? That's where the real teaching lives.

Your kids don't need a perfectly calm parent. They need one who shows that emotions are normal, that mistakes happen, and that love doesn't pack its bags just because things got messy. Learning how to reconnect after a rupture might be one of the most powerful lessons they'll ever get from you.

Q5: What if I don't even know what I feel most of the time?

I have the word "human" scribbled on a Post-it on my computer, because even after all the tools and all the reading and training, I still catch myself thinking, *Come on, Leonora, you should know better.* But often, I don't. I'm in it too.

To help, gently ask yourself: *What am I really feeling? What do I need? What story am I telling myself?* Even if you don't have the answers, just asking those questions gives you something to hold onto. As Djokovic said, "The more you practise being present, the quicker you bounce back when you need to."

Q6: How long will it take to feel like I'm getting this right?

Let's take "right" off the table. This isn't about becoming a flawless, all-knowing parent. It's about becoming a truer version of yourself, one who shows up, feels deeply, and is willing to grow alongside your children. Besides, if you were aiming for perfect parenting, you're reading the wrong book.

Q7: Can I do this even if my partner isn't on the same page?

You absolutely can. It starts with one person showing up differently, and that alone can shift the atmosphere in a home. Your tone, your regulation, and your willingness to pause and reflect will create ripples. Even if they don't speak the language of feelings (yet), they'll feel the impact of your steady presence. This is about modelling what it looks like to do the inner work and letting the rest unfold in its own time.

Q8: What if I try to connect emotionally, and my child just shrugs and walks off?

Then congratulations, you've just had a perfectly normal parenting experience. Don't let it deter you. Connection isn't always visible in the moment. Sometimes your calm presence lands hours later, when they're lying in bed or lobbing socks at their sibling.

Keep showing up and doing the work. Emotional seeds take time to sprout, but they do.

ESPECIALLY FOR YOU

Parenting beside someone is both a gift and a mirror. It shows you the best of love, and the parts of yourself you'd rather not see.

Before I go any further, I want to say something to those doing this alone. I can't pretend to know exactly what that's like, but I've listened, watched, and sat beside women who shoulder it all. The strength that takes is relentless. What I'm about to share speaks from partnership, but please don't hear exclusion. The connection, reflection, and courage to keep showing up are the same, no matter what your family looks like.

If you are parenting alongside someone, you'll know that teamwork isn't always the picture of harmony. Some days it flows, other days it falls flat, and sometimes it feels like you're both dancing to different songs entirely. That's normal. What I've learned is that the real growth doesn't happen in the big, obvious moments; it's tucked inside the quiet ones, the subtle exchanges, the sighs you both pretend not to hear, and the times one of you reaches out while the other quietly pulls away.

When you start paying attention to those in-between moments, something shifts. You begin to notice not just what's happening between you, but what's happening inside you, too. Because emotions don't stay put. They're like toddlers with scissors. Give them a second, and they'll make their presence known. They spill out in ways we don't plan—through that tone we swear sounds perfectly normal (it doesn't), or the sigh we pass off as a casual exhale when it's really the sound of your body saying, *Enough already!*

You can tell yourself you're fine all you like, but your body's already out there performing a one-woman show called *Absolutely Not Fine...*

When I'm fed up but pretending otherwise, it's painfully obvious. My arms cross, my jaw sets, and I start clattering dishes like a woman auditioning for *Stomp*. Everyone in the house knows what's up. I might not be saying it out loud, but I am communicating, *I am not happy with you people*. And let me tell you, this is not something I do from the hidey hole. Oh no, no. For this kind of performance, I like an audience.

A couple of nights ago, I escaped to my home office to write. The thing about working from home is that it's dangerously easy to disappear into it, especially when you love what you do. And I do. Plus, I'd hit my limit with *Modern Family* and was happy to let Neil and our seventeen-year-old son deal with yet another Dunphy crisis.

Five minutes later, he called up, "Are you coming?"

"Five minutes!" I shouted back. The most flexible five minutes in history.

Half an hour later, he'd switched off the TV, stomped upstairs, and announced he was going to bed. (For the record, we are never in bed at nine p.m.)

What I didn't know was that he wanted to talk. He turned off the TV, waited, and then felt irritated that I kept disappearing without saying where I was or what I was doing. There we were, he irritated, not really knowing why, and I irritated that he was irritated, because from my point of view, *What on earth was the big deal?*

Maybe that sounds familiar. You and your partner are circling each other, both a little defensive and neither quite sure why. You want to connect, but your emotions get there first. And when you don't stop to notice what's going on, those emotions find a way out in other ways.

One may snap, the other may be infuriatingly reasonable (both are easier than feeling). This dance is part of every long-term partnership, two nervous systems trying to find safety at the same time.

To make matters worse, you might be the one at home, raising the children while quietly carrying the invisible weight of everything else. The meals, the laundry, the calendar, and the emotional temperature of the whole house all somehow end up on you.

You know your partner's working hard too, but when they walk through the door, it doesn't always feel even.

They go to work, come home to more work, and by the time the kids are finally asleep, it's as if you become the work. You're ready for the "evening download"—not a heart-to-heart exactly, more a verbal spreadsheet with columns for emotional labour, energy output, and unacknowledged achievements.

You both know you've been putting out fires in your own ways, but when you're disconnected from yourself, you can't always see that. You can't even find the words: "I'm tired because …"; "I'm anxious about …"; "I just need five minutes." Instead, you hand over fragments and hope he'll piece them together. How could he, when half the time you haven't decoded them yourself?

Partnership isn't supposed to be about who does more, though on bad days that's exactly how it feels. It's meant to be a team sport: not just shared chores, but shared truth. The kind where you say the real thing instead of expecting your partner to decode the sighs, the silences, and the "I'm fine" that obviously means the opposite.

It helps when both people are willing to do the work. But if your partner isn't there yet, that's not your failure. As Mel Robbins says, it's a *Let Them* moment. Let them be where they are. Let them feel what they feel. You stay on your side of the fence, tending what's yours.

This isn't about changing them. It's about the one thing you can influence: you. Your awareness, your patterns, and your responses. Doing the work on your side isn't surrender;

it's self-respect. When you start to see what's really going on for you, the blame eases, the resentment loses its edge, and slowly, the whole atmosphere in the house shifts, not because they've changed, but because you have.

Instead of keeping invisible scoreboards (which I did for years), the real work begins when you start asking about the feeling behind the feeling. That's where everything lives. Those inner conversations won't come naturally at first. You won't voice your needs; you'll expect your partner to guess them; when they guess wrong (which they probably will), you'll be tempted to tell yourself, *They don't understand; they aren't even trying.* And just to round things off nicely, *They don't care.*

While I'd love to say that partnership involves sharing emotions through some kind of romantic osmosis, where one look across the kitchen somehow communicates, *I'm emotionally depleted, please bring tea and validation,* it doesn't work that way. The next step after checking in with yourself is sharing those inner thoughts with your partner, out loud, and with words.

Instead of saying, "I need a break," try, "I'm feeling overwhelmed, and I need some space." Instead of, "You never help," try, "I'm starting to feel invisible, and that's hard to carry." Naming the emotion underneath the reaction moves you both out of blame and into connection.

It doesn't take grand sit-downs, just tiny moments of truth in the middle of the chaos. A passing comment in the hallway, or an exhale on the couch once the kids are finally asleep. Those small exchanges whisper, *Let's not lose each other in the noise.*

Real teamwork isn't about flawless juggling; it's about picking up the dropped balls together and remembering that even the best teams need practice. And that's really what this is about—practising how to listen to yourself, to understand what you're carrying, and to do the same for the person beside you.

That's the work of emotional growth: noticing, understanding, and trying again. It's what will steady you, and it's what your children will learn to stand on, long after you've stopped reminding them how.

FINAL THOUGHTS

If you've made it through the quiet unravelling, the truth-telling, and the little toe-dips into the slightly woo-woo, take a second to breathe that in. You didn't just read this; you showed up for yourself. You noticed, remembered, and maybe even faced something you usually sidestep. That's huge, and only the beginning.

When I first began this work, I thought the job was to help my kids name their feelings, stay calm, and manage the big waves. I poured myself into that, but while I was teaching them emotional awareness, I was sidestepping my own. None of us can, and that's why this section comes first. Before we can help our children navigate their emotions, we have to be brave enough to sit with our own.

The turning point was realising that my kids didn't need a mother who was endlessly composed, but one who was aware of her own needs. One who could say, "I'm struggling right now," instead of snapping and not knowing why. I understood then that the only way to teach them the value of emotional expression was to live it, to show that feelings are safe, that they have something to tell us, and that when we listen, we get to choose how we respond.

So, what changes when you start doing this inner work? Wouldn't it be nice if there were a certificate at the end? "Congratulations, you've completed 10,000 hours of noticing your feelings and may now proceed to eternal calm." Let's be clear, there's no finish line, no enlightenment badge, and definitely no applause. Change happens in tiny, invisible moments: the pause before reacting, the breath before snapping, the apology that comes a little quicker than before. That progress tells you that you're on the right path.

I first recognised change when the chaos inside me began to match the calm I'd been pretending to have on the outside. My family noticed before I did. Neil and the kids have all said, in their own ways, that my mood sets the tone of the house. I used to take that as pressure; now I take it as a compliment. When I'm anchored, they feel safer to drift and come back again. My calm doesn't fix everything, but it gives everyone a place to land, and that's the real change.

I've seen it in myself, too. I'm calmer, less rollercoaster, and only slightly dramatic about misplaced shoes. I still lose the plot sometimes, but the space between unravelling and repair is shorter now, and that's what progress looks like.

I've seen the same in the women I work with. As they reconnect with themselves, their homes shift, their children relax, and their relationships breathe again. That's the quiet miracle of this work: it doesn't just change what you do; it changes the atmosphere you live in.

From here, we move into the real stuff, where theory meets the school run, toddler tantrums, teenage moods, and the occasional emotional explosion (mine included). None of it's neat, but all of it's honest. Together, we'll walk it one messy, meaningful moment at a time, and see where this presence thing leads.

FOR SKIM LOVERS

If you've landed here, I'm guessing you've either read the entire section and want a brief reminder of what it's about, or you are experiencing emotional overload and want the highlights.

You're in the right place. This section is not a summary of everything, but it will give you an overview of what we've covered.

You don't have to keep it all in.

Just because no one asked doesn't mean your feelings don't count.

Unspoken emotions don't vanish; they wait, and they wear you down.

You are more than the calm you perform.

The polished version of you might get through the day, but she's not the whole story.

There's value in letting the real you surface, the one who isn't always fine.

Your inner world matters.

Even when the to-do list screams louder, and it feels like no one's noticing.

Tuning into yourself isn't indulgent; it's essential.

Feeling doesn't make you fragile.

You can be competent and cracking a little. You can be grateful and grieving.

There's space for both. Always has been.

You don't need to be perfect.

What your kids need isn't flawless; it's honest.

They need to see what it looks like to feel something and stay present through it.

You're allowed to be in this story too.

Motherhood doesn't mean disappearing. It's not about being exclusive to your kids' emotional needs. It's about including yourself in the equation, on purpose and without guilt.

THE TAKEAWAY:

You are allowed to take up space in your own story.

Emotional connection starts with you, your needs, your truth, and your presence.

That's the part your kids remember, and the part that brings you back home to yourself.

Part II

Navigating Toddler Emotions

THE HEART OF THE TODDLER

The first part was all about *us*, because if we can get that part even slightly right, everything that follows (including the emotional whirlwind of toddlerhood) becomes a little easier to survive.

And mark my words, you'll want to do more than just survive. When it comes to toddlers, there will be tears, food in impossible places, and moments when you'll genuinely wonder if you're raising a feral raccoon. Actually, can I just backtrack for a moment? Have you ever marvelled at how much food one small human can wedge into every crevice of a highchair? That clean-up operation nearly drove me insane. Sorry, I know that's a bit random, but I had to mention it.

What I want to say is that this ride is a messy one. And I'm not talking about the highchair this time, but the emotional rollercoaster that comes with a toddler's development.

When they arrive, control becomes something from another life. You can meditate, journal, and breathe until your eyelashes flutter. Still, all it takes is one cereal spill or a meltdown over the wrong spoon, and every bit of learning from the "investing in you" part of this book packs its bags and leaves without a second glance.

This is easily done, of course, because toddlers seem to be the undisputed world champions of emotion. By the age of three, they've explored the entire emotional spectrum from every possible angle and paired each feeling with a set of sound effects they've been perfecting since birth. The challenge, as every parent knows, is that toddlers don't yet have the words or the social graces to go with those emotions. Most of it is just trying to find a way out of a body that's still learning what to do with it all.

Instead of focusing on that, we tend to fixate on our need to have good children. Because somewhere along the line, we decided that good children equal good parents.

That right there is some seriously skewed thinking, the point where we accidentally conflate morality with healthy development.

Our little people don't behave the way they do because they're tiny rebels in training. They behave that way because, by design, their brains are still immature.

And yet, at the age of three, we expect them to do things like share. Sharing is important, obviously. But they have no idea how to. It will be years before their neural wiring gives them that ability. Yet here we are, scolding them for not passing the Duplo and then wondering why we've raised generations of adults who feel like they're never quite enough.

Our job isn't to bring them in line, or to pray their outbursts don't end up on TikTok; it's to stay calm and model emotional maturity. Well, that's the plan. In reality, I usually make it about four seconds before muttering something unprintable and bribing them with a snack. Let's not pretend I'm alone in this. Snacks are a universal currency for all mothers of toddlers everywhere.

If we think back to *ourselves* for a moment, we've agreed that when we resist or ignore our emotions, they don't simply disappear; they try to get our attention in a different way. We've also talked about how, if we pause long enough to listen, they give us a clearer understanding of what's happening inside and what might help next.

The same applies to our children. But they can't do it alone. They need us to help them make sense of what's happening inside *them* and love them while we're doing it. If we don't, their emotions will circle back, louder, stronger, and more desperate to be seen. I know because I was outnumbered by three living, breathing case studies for years.

There are two things I want to say before we continue. First, the examples ahead don't always show me at my best. At the time, I didn't have the tools or the insight I do now, so what follows is really a compilation of my greatest hits in "what not to do." I'm sharing them as a learning moment, not a self-critique, because believe me, I've done plenty of that already.

Second, I feel I owe toddlers a kind of public service announcement. Before diving into what can only be described as their beautiful chaos, it seems only fair to acknowledge their absolute cuteness. Let's face it, most of what they do and say is *heart-meltingly adorable.* The first time they say a word, grab your hand as they take their first steps, or wear socks on their hands for reasons known only to them, your whole heart melts into a puddle of pure love. In that moment, you forget the sleep deprivation and think, *Yes, this is the best thing that's ever happened to me.*

My oldest went through a phase where she wore a bucket on her head, handle tucked neatly under her chin like a helmet strap, to the grocery store. Playing the part of the embarrassed parent, I was secretly bursting with pride. She absolutely owned that bucket. Then, almost overnight, those sweet, harmless quirks gave way to something louder and far less Insta-worthy. The glory days of the bucket were replaced by protests that could bring an entire car park to a standstill simply because I dared to sing along to her favourite song. *I mean, really, what on earth possessed me to think I could join in? As if my slightly off-key attempt could ever measure up to hers. Rookie mistake.*

That same child who once cooed sweetly in my arms would become inconsolable because I handed her juice in a red cup instead of a blue one. What is it with the colours? She didn't even know their names yet, but somehow knew I'd committed an unforgivable error. The eruption that followed defied all logic, like Newton forgot to mention the toddler law of emotional force: the smaller the body, the greater the impact of its fury. Was it the cup, the drink, or are we still circling back to the singing incident? You'll never know, and that's the part every mother recognises, the helpless head-scratching as the meltdown runs its course.

For the most part, there's little middle ground with toddlers. Everything is either the best thing ever or the absolute worst. It's kind of baffling. The speed of the fluctuations is something to behold. One minute, you're basking in the glow of being the best parent who ever lived. Sixty seconds later, they're devastated that today's snack is an apple instead of a banana, because heaven forbid you change the routine without advance warning.

Apple? Oh no. How dare you?! Cue the shouting, the fake tears, and the dramatic roll across the floor. "Fine, banana then." Deep breath. Giggles. Hugs. "Mommy, I love you and want to live with you forever." And just like that, the storm passes, and you're thinking, *Call off child services, everyone's fine, promise.*

I recently read an article that described tantrums as an "exciting stage" of child development. I'm sorry, but no. There is nothing exciting about peeling your child off a grocery store floor because you said no for the twenty-seven thousandth time to, "Can I have …?" Sometimes I wonder what would happen if we just said yes to everything. "Sure, toss in the chocolate cereal, the novelty biscuits, and the economy pack of lollipops. Why not the family-size tub of ice cream, too? Okay, buddy, now you push the trolley."

These outbursts are one loud chapter in the unpredictable journey of learning to feel and find the words that match that feeling. For a moment, all of it's lost in translation. That must be incredibly challenging.

Imagine you wake up in a foreign country with no phone, no internet, and not a single clue where you are. You're exhausted, starving, and need the toilet. You try to ask for help, using what you *think* are the right words, but the person you're speaking to just smiles politely and hands you a sandwich. You try again, a bit louder this time, adding some wild hand gestures for good measure, and now they're offering you a chair and pointing at the sky. You scream, "No, that's not what I mean!" But the words don't come out right, so instead you cry, or maybe you throw your hands in the air, or maybe you just give up and sit on the pavement, because what's the point anymore?

That's what it must be like for toddlers. They're trying to tell us something, but it's coming out all wrong. We keep handing them sandwiches when they're really saying, *This is too much for me, and I don't know how to handle it.*

I remember standing in a U.S. border security queue, three children circling, and my patience dangling by a thread. If you've ever been through U.S. border control, you'll know that the lines stretch forever, even at two a.m. Joshua, at three, took one look at the body scanner and staged a full-scale protest. His pushchair had vanished on the conveyor, and as far as he was concerned, that was the path he should be taking too.

He sobbed, wailed, and twisted out of every attempt I made to soothe him, while my older two offered constant updates about how we were *definitely* going to miss our next flight. Sweat gathered under my shirt, and I could feel the weight of a hundred weary eyes judging us from the queue. In that moment, it felt as though we alone were holding up the entire U.S. border. His emotions were loud and unfiltered, and mine ran just beneath the surface, hidden but no less real.

Now, I'm assuming you've read Part 1 and nodded along to all my talk about "being present with your feelings." If so, you might be tempted to fling this book out the nearest window right about now—because if someone had handed *me* this book in that airport security queue, I'd have thrown it straight back. Presence sounds lovely in theory, until you're the one sweating through border control with a screaming toddler.

I wasn't thinking about breathwork or mindfulness; present-moment awareness was more like: *Find the exit now!* The reality is that I was an exhausted parent who had just spent nine hours trying to entertain three young children on an international flight. I was so drained that the idea of lying down on the conveyor belt myself was starting to sound reasonable.

Meanwhile, I was furious that Josh couldn't understand that the pushchair would come back. I felt irrationally offended by the security guard, who looked at us as though we'd tried to smuggle a small zoo through customs. And I was livid with Neil, who, to be clear, was being nothing but supportive, but since I didn't have the tools to reset, blaming someone felt like the only option.

"You're not helping," I hissed under my breath. Then, "Why don't you do something?" And because I couldn't stop myself, "Also, you cut the cake wrong at the pirate party five years ago." The poor man didn't stand a chance. In that moment, his chewing was too loud, his breathing was wrong, and honestly, his very existence was just... too much. Which, of course, was utterly ridiculous. But try telling that to my nervous system, which clearly needed someone to blame. Why is it that the more overwhelmed we are, the less grip we have on reality? (*Note to self: Apologise to Neil. Properly. Maybe with cake... cut correctly this time.*)

Here's where the advice columns would say, "Pause and ground yourself." You know the drill: 5-4-3-2-1, what can you see, touch, smell? Not happening. Gratitude practice? You're joking. Feel the sensation of your fingertips? Seriously?

By some small miracle, and a lot of deep breathing, I did manage to coax Joshua through that scanner while asking myself if I'd really expected him to say, "Mom, I'm feeling a little anxious and disoriented, and I don't quite understand where my pushchair is going. Could you please clarify?" As if.

When you zoom out a little, the whole thing starts to make sense. Tantrums aren't proof that your child is possessed; they're just part of the growing-up curriculum. Our job isn't to fix it or hush it; it's to help them figure out what they're feeling and how to say it without flattening us in the process.

I know that all sounds very wise, blah blah blah, cue the soothing background music. The reality is that this stuff is hard. I have been the parent doing the deep breathing while silently questioning every decision I've ever made. But I've also done the work I'm writing about, so I know that both can be true.

When we meet our children where they are, instead of where we wish they were, things really do go better. If we can see that their confusion is an invitation to learn with them, not control them, the whole experience begins to shift, and the rewards of that shift are powerful. These are the moments that build trust and belonging, and they're worth remembering.

It's why I want to share these stories with you, not polished "how-tos," but the raw, honest accounts of what it looked like when I didn't have a clue. Those moments, awkward and uncomfortable as they were, became my greatest teachers. If we can soften the story we tell about "tantrum toddlers" and begin to see those meltdowns for what they really are, we open the door to a connection that goes far deeper than we ever expected.

But knowing something in theory and living it in the chaos of real life are two very different things. The lessons that shaped me most came not from calm reflection, but from the messy, unfiltered moments of motherhood. One of those moments had crumbs, tears, and a muffin at its centre.

THE MUFFINGATE SCANDAL

You've already met Josh, the self-appointed spokesperson for the rights of pushchairs USA, but now I'd like to *properly* introduce you.

Josh arrived in the world six years after his brother and eight after his sister, which basically meant I'd cracked the whole parenting thing. I was calm, capable, and still under the illusion that I was in control of our home, routines, and, to a certain degree, everyone's emotions.

Around that time, I'd treated myself to a label maker. It was one of those gadgets I'd always secretly wanted. I found it oddly exciting to label the jars, drawers, school folders, and even the kitchen plug sockets. Admittedly, it couldn't label what was going on *inside* me, but it did a fine job of making everything else look orderly. That was close enough.

So, by the time Josh came along, I'd filed and labelled my way into believing I'd mastered motherhood. I was more than ready for Take Three. Or so I liked to think.

Josh had other plans.

He arrived like a determined whirlwind, full of energy and curiosity and absolutely no interest in my carefully labelled systems. At five months, he skipped crawling entirely and launched himself into a wobbly shuffle that seemed part ambition, and part near-death experience. If there was a ball in sight, he'd throw himself at it like a stuntman, sometimes crashing and laughing, sometimes collapsing in a heap of frustration before immediately trying again. I lived on high alert, one hand permanently ready to catch him.

At six months, he abruptly ended my milkmaid career. No warning, no gradual transition, just a decisive, *Thanks, but I'm done here.* I sat there, slightly stunned, and feeling weirdly rejected.

Parenting him left me constantly teetering between awe and exhaustion. It's hard to explain how someone so small, with cheeks that squish like marshmallows, could hold so much power. It was only a matter of time before baked goods became one of our biggest battlegrounds.

Enter Muffingate... the day chaos became curriculum.

I had invited a new acquaintance over for coffee. Everything was scrubbed, polished, and cleaned, and Josh and I were making muffins. He took his job seriously, stirring with great concentration and licking the spoon with even greater enthusiasm. When the muffins came out of the oven, we stood there, side by side, proud of our efforts and quietly enjoying what had been a perfect morning.

Then, as the smell of warm muffins filled the kitchen, he looked up at me, wide-eyed and hopeful. "Can I have one now, Mommy?" he asked, the very picture of politeness. My heart swelled with pride. *Look at me, raising a child who asks so nicely.* I may even have given myself a tiny, invisible pat on the back, and for a second, almost caved. He had done all the work, after all. (Well, mostly.) But no, this was about appearances, remember, and we were being civilised. I smiled and said, "Not yet, sweetheart, we'll wait for our guest."

He blinked at me as though I'd just cancelled Christmas. His expression shifted from confusion and then to quiet disbelief, as if trying to decide whether I'd completely lost my mind. Josh was three, after all, and had little patience for hospitality or social niceties. What mattered were the muffins he'd made with his own two hands.

Before long, he was pacing the kitchen like a pint-sized security guard, eyes locked on the cooling rack, issuing status updates every thirty seconds. "Is she here yet... what about now?"

By the time the doorbell rang, he was already starting to unravel, and the moment she stepped inside, he made his move, straight for the biggest muffin. Before he'd even finished his last bite, he looked up at me, cheeks covered in crumbs, and asked, "Can I have another?" Fair question. They were good muffins, and really, when is one ever enough? But, yet again, I said no. It's what a person in control is supposed to say, isn't it? One more muffin wouldn't have ruined the day or my reputation as a host. It was just

a muffin. Yet somehow, in that moment, it felt like everything rested on my ability to prove I was in charge, which I
clearly was not, because seconds later, his little body trem-
bled. Down he went into a full cinematic collapse, complete
with sound effects. Spielberg himself couldn't have directed
it better.

While his emotions exploded across the floor, mine sim-
mered just below the surface. I let out that overly bright
laugh parents use to say, *He's just having a moment,* when
what we really mean is, *Please, God, let the floor swallow me
whole.*

Most mothers know the embarrassment of a moment
like this. My son wasn't "performing" the way I thought
he should, and I could feel my composure slipping. I was
angry that he'd ruined our morning, ashamed that I cared
so much, and anxious about what my guest must be thinking. Notice I didn't mention poor Josh in that list.

So, what now? That's the question every parent faces in
moments like these. Looking back, I almost wish I'd turned
to my guest and said, "Do me a favour, love, could you just
sit with him while I consult my inner self and consider the
appropriate response?" Sadly, there's never time for that
sort of calm introspection, and with patience running thin,
I turned to Josh and hissed, "Calm down."

It was a command meant entirely for him, but the
irony was that I probably needed to hear it more. Instead,
I pressed on, "If you don't pull yourself together, you're

going to your room." Unsurprisingly, this made everything worse. He cried louder, stomped harder, and then went full spaghetti mode right there on the floor, a living, thrashing demonstration of the "motion" in emotions.

Five minutes dragged on like fifty, and finally, with no plan and even less patience, I scooped him up mid-wail and marched him off to his room.

"You stay here until you can behave," I snapped, shutting the door with more force than I meant to. Behave? What did that even mean? Stay here... until when? Until he was calm? Until dinner? Until he turned eighteen?

The truth is, he *had* behaved. He'd waited, he'd asked, and he'd held it together as long as any three-year-old possibly could. Then, when his little nervous system gave out, he fell apart, and in my frustration, so did I, punctuating it all with a door slam. Did I stop to wonder what his cries might really be saying? Of course not. I saw disobedience, and I wasn't willing to accept it.

Now I wonder, did Josh, a mindfulness guru in disguise, pause for a few breaths and emerge regulated? That's what three-year-olds do, right? They find their inner zen, calm their nervous system, and bounce back.

Not a chance.

He didn't sit on the edge of his bed and quietly reflect on the finer points of self-control. Instead, he screamed louder, kicked harder, and sobbed until he was hiccupping, demanding muffin justice like a tiny activist whose human

rights had been violated. The more he cried, the more determined I was to stand my ground. "No muffin for you, and
you can stay in there all day," I muttered. *Maybe forever.* I
didn't say it out loud, but I thought it.

When I think back to that day, it still hurts. Who was I
then? What was I trying to prove, and to whom? Looking
at it now, it was just one reaction piled on top of another,
none of it making any real sense. If I'd stopped, even for a
breath, I might have noticed how awful my own responses
were making me feel and realised that Josh was feeling it
too. The difference was, he let his out, and I hid mine. I
thought composure made me strong, but really, it just made
me unreachable to the person who needed me most. When
I finally opened the door, it wasn't with a white flag; it was
as if someone was still clinging to control, hoping it might
somehow redeem the situation. "Are you ready?" I asked.

Ready? That's right up there with "just behave" and
"calm down." The absurdity of it makes me cringe even
now. Ready for what, exactly? A civil debate? A peace
treaty? A nap schedule scribbled in muffin crumbs? Once
again, he was three. He wasn't weighing up his readiness;
he was drowning in emotions he had no idea how to escape.
It pains me to think that I never once stopped to consider
what he was trying to tell me, which is ridiculous given how
fiercely he was trying to be heard. Josh wasn't clutching a
muffin; he was clutching his heart, holding it out in plain

sight, begging me to see how much it mattered. All I had to offer in return was a slammed door that told him I didn't.

I didn't understand that his outburst wasn't rebellion or tiredness, explanations I often used to smooth over big emotions. It was his way of saying, *I'm struggling. I don't understand. Please help me.* He was speaking the only language he had. If I'd really listened, I might have realised that he needed me to help him make sense of what he was feeling. I was his person, after all, but when I shut that door, what he saw instead was, *Actually, she's not.*

I'm about 110% sure that if a close friend of mine had a mini meltdown, I wouldn't shut the door on her. I'd sit beside her, pass her tissues, and say, "I know. It's a lot. Tell me everything." Yet there I was, choosing to see his behaviour as naughtiness.

If I'd paused long enough to notice what was really happening, I might have asked myself the same questions I now ask others: *What's actually going on here? What are you hoping your actions will achieve?* Clearly, whatever I was doing wasn't working. What I needed was to turn to my guest and say, "There's something he's trying to tell me, and it's just coming out wrong. I'm going to step into his world, and we'll figure it out together." And maybe, I'd have added, "… so that he doesn't have to spend the next twenty years figuring it out for himself."

I was reminded of this recently while listening to Mel Robbins interview psychologist Dr Stuart Ablon, who said,

"People do well if they can." Not if they *want* to. If they *can*.

It sounds simple, but it invites us to look at our hearts and see what's really there. Mine says I love my children with my whole heart and want the very best for them. That's what I *want*. But wanting doesn't mean it will always happen. It doesn't mean I'll show up as my best self every time, or that they will. We do well if we can, if we have the tools, the mindset, and the support to help us. The same goes for our children. They will do well if they can, if they have parents who are learning alongside them, who are patient and kind, and who can get it wrong and try again. That, really, is the heart of what Dr Ablon was saying.

So, what if, instead of criticising ourselves for not knowing, we learned to listen? To meet our own hearts with curiosity instead of judgement, and with presence instead of pressure? Maybe that's where real change begins in moments like Muffingate, when we finally start to see what's happening underneath.

NOT MY FINEST HOUR

Growth doesn't come from trying harder or judging ourselves into being better. It comes from looking straight at
the moments we'd rather bury and saying, *I see it now. I
wish I'd done it differently. Next time, I will.*

I was reminded of this today while coaching a mother
who'd argued with her son about going to school. He'd felt
dizzy after rugby practice, but she sent him anyway. By
lunchtime, the school called to say he might have a concus-
sion. She'd known he needed rest, but in that moment, she
chose what she needed instead. The result was a healthy
dose of guilt and the familiar chorus of "I'm not good
enough" playing in the background.

As she spoke, I just watched quietly and thought, *You
and a hundred thousand other mothers have felt this too.* We all
carry moments like these, the ones that cling, whispering
what we should have done differently. These heavy feelings
have a way of unpacking their bags and making themselves
right at home, so the trick is to acknowledge them, name
them, and gently show them the door. I often remind my
clients, and myself, to hold it lightly. When we grip guilt
and regret like they're proof of failure, they only grow

heavier, but when we hold them lightly, they become teachers instead of tenants.

Take Muffingate—at the time, I thought it was just a disaster involving baked goods and poor judgement, but it was the moment I began learning how to turn what felt heavy into something that could finally move me forward.

Looking back, I see that I was ...

Expecting too much.

The hardest thing to face, even now, is how much was expected of Josh. I wanted him to meet me in the calm, tidy version of the world I was trying to create. I wanted him to manage his emotions with the composure I couldn't find in myself. Which is laughable, really, given this was a tiny human still learning how to balance on one leg and hold a spoon without catapulting yoghurt across the room. "Are you ready?" I asked, as though readiness was something a three-year-old could measure or even pronounce.

Toddlers live entirely in the moment. That's their job. Josh was doing exactly that, happily submerged in his muffins, while I was expecting him to step neatly out of his world and into mine. I wanted him to notice the crumbs, remember his manners, and prioritise my guest's comfort over his own excitement. It was ridiculous.

The truth is, I was asking him to regulate emotions I couldn't even regulate myself. That was the fundamental mismatch. He was being exactly who he was meant to be, three years old, messy, present, gloriously unfiltered, and I was holding him to standards he couldn't possibly meet.

Shutting the story and silencing the noise.

When I look back at that morning, I can see that for Josh, the whole thing was one long, glorious, sugar-coated story. From lining up the ingredients to sifting, stirring, and the mandatory licking, he was completely absorbed. Gazing through the oven door, waiting for the magic to happen, was the final chapter before the fairytale ending of eating what he had created.

What he wasn't expecting was the wicked witch of the West (or was it the East?) swooping in to cut the story short. When he tried to tell me, in his own toddler way, through noise, I didn't hear it. I just silenced him.

Now I know emotions are simply messages about unmet needs. It was Josh's way of saying, *I'm confused. I don't understand why this is happening, and I have no idea how long your mysterious guest is going to take.* I didn't see that. I thought the story was about good manners, guest etiquette, and keeping up appearances. In that, I did what so many of us do; I ended the story with a slam of the door that echoed, *I'll decide the ending, thanks.*

Missing the invitation.

Every emotional storm carries an invitation. That morning, Josh was inviting me into his world. What I saw as an outburst, an act of defiance, was a cry for connection. I stood tall when what he needed was for me to crouch beside him and help him make sense of feelings that were far too big for his little body to hold.

If we talk about needs, those were his. He needed me to be kind, understanding, and compassionate, especially in the storm; he needed to hear, "Let's work this out together."

That's the invitation I missed.

Performing for the guest.

That morning, my guest's comfort mattered more to me than my son's feelings. I wanted her to think I was one of those calm, capable mothers who could handle anything, the kind who doesn't lose her cool even when muffins are flying across the kitchen.

In the end, she got a front-row seat to the chaos, and Josh got lost in the background. His story, pride, and need to be seen were all sacrificed so I could look like I had it together.

I've done that many times, chosen to look okay instead of being okay. It's such a common pattern for mothers, isn't it? We keep performing, hoping someone will finally believe we're enough, when really, what we need most is to believe it ourselves.

I missed a lot that morning, but missing it made me pay closer attention in the moments that came after. It forced me to notice how toddlers reach for connection with the few tools they have, and how easily those tools can be overlooked when we're caught up in appearances.

There is something natural about wanting to make a good impression, to set things out neatly, and to show the world we're doing okay, and that's fine, but toddlers don't see any of that. In Joshua's world that day, it was him, me, and a muffin. That was all.

We're not meant to parent like robots, calmly handling every outburst as though we've memorised a script. We're meant to meet our little people right where they are, at the beginning of their emotional journey.

This was not my finest hour; I can own that, but I'm also grateful for it. That one experience has become something I return to often. It shaped how I think about the way young children process emotions and reminds me why their stories matter just as much as our own.

What do I wish I'd done instead? Plenty. And that's where I want to take you next—to the place where connection begins to grow, even out of the most muffin-crumbled moments.

IF I COULD DO IT OVER

If offered a do-over, would I skip the muffins altogether? Tempting. But they were just the props. The real drama was what was going on beneath the flour and the feelings. To get to the heart of the matter, let's treat this as a post-project review: What worked; what bombed; what needs tweaking? It's the benefit of hindsight—it gives us a look at how we might handle it better in the future.

If I could do it over, I would...

Choose my battle.

Muffingate was never about sugar, or dinner, or even manners; it was about timing. Some moments just aren't the place for parenting wisdom. That was one of them. Rather than turning a baked good into a battleground, I should have handed him the muffin, watched his face light up, and saved the lesson on etiquette for another day.

The same logic could be applied to the airport security queue. Joshua was sleep-deprived, overstimulated, and confused about the disappearance of his pushchair. That is *definitely* the time for a snack bribe, not a lesson. Have a piece of chocolate yourself while you're at it. Keep your dignity. Try again tomorrow.

Set the right standards.

It would have behoved me to soften the standards I was holding, not just for Joshua, but for myself too. I was using words that made sense in my adult world, where logic and reason and polite explanations tend to work, assuming they would somehow translate into toddler language. They didn't. He wasn't being defiant; he was being three. How could I expect him to regulate emotions I could barely regulate myself? That's not fair.

Also, and let's be real here, have you *always* modelled etiquette and patience when there's a tray of niceties on display? I haven't. Not even close. Enough said.

Rethink the priority.

Who do you think mattered most in that moment? Was it Josh, flat on the floor, feelings exposed? Was it me, holding my breath behind a slammed door? Or was it the guest in the lounge, sipping coffee, and possibly grading my performance? The answer should be obvious.

Yet, she was my priority. I put her comfort and happiness ahead of my son's emotional world, and that part is hard to admit. What really should have counted was showing Josh that his feelings mattered more than anything else. If I could relive it, I'd have said to the guest (or anyone, for that matter), "Give me a minute; he needs me right now." Maybe she'd have respected that more. I know I would have respected myself more for it.

Choose presence over perfection.

Perfection had me scrubbing floors, silencing meltdowns, and holding everything together so nothing would fall apart. Presence would have asked me to stop holding and start seeing the small, trembling face in front of me, waiting for me to notice. To say, "I hear you and I'm here."

Perfection is about how it looks, while presence is about how it feels. That day, I mistook control for care. If I'd chosen presence, I might have softened and found his voice beneath my own.

Validate feelings.

I don't know about you, but I know exactly how it feels when someone shuts me down mid-feeling. It only makes the feelings bigger, doesn't it? Like you need to shout just to be heard. That's what I did to Josh. I couldn't see that his feelings made sense in their own way, just as mine did. We were both overwhelmed, just speaking different languages.

If I could do it over, I wouldn't have rushed to talk about behaviour or consequences. I would have sat beside him, looked into his tear-streaked face, and tried to name the disappointment I saw. Maybe that simple act of recognising what he was trying to tell me, and how much it mattered to him, would have softened the moment for both of us.

Practise the pause.

If I could do it over, I'd start with a breath. A real one. Deep in, slow out.

I can process a lot in a single breath. Dinner plans, shopping lists, who's coming, at what time, and who still needs to be told. All in one inhale. That's motherhood for you.

If I'd used that breath back then, I could have done the quick Leonora check-in:

What's actually going on here? What do I need? What does he need? What would make sense right now? Instead, I went straight into reaction mode, which is never my finest strategy.

Notice, it's "practising" the pause. There are two bits involved: the pause and the practice. The pause gives you a bit of breathing room; the practice is what stops you from forgetting it next time. None of it happens overnight. It takes a hundred imperfect pauses, a thousand deep breaths, and a bit of persistence before it starts to feel even remotely natural.

There are so many "if I could do it again" moments in parenting. What matters most is building a foundation of safety and trust you both can return to when things get too big. That's what gives our children the courage to feel deeply, and the confidence to know they're never alone in it.

In the end, it's the relationship that matters most, and the lesson we want our children to carry.

WHAT I LEARNED

So much of parenting happens on the surface. We react to what we can see, when what's really shaping the moment is what we can't.

For a long time, I've followed the work of Dr Vanessa Lapointe, a child psychologist who says that behaviour is only ever the tip of the iceberg. The real work is what's happening beneath the surface. I love that. It takes the pressure off trying to fix every outburst or meltdown and turns the focus towards what's really going on inside the small human (and, let's be honest, the big human too).

What she taught me is that most of us are trained to stop at the surface. We see the shove, the shout, the pounding fists, and we go straight into "make it stop" mode. We call it discipline, but often it's just panic in a slightly more respectable outfit. We confiscate the iPad, send them to their room, or issue that classic parental line: "I'm taking away something you love." It's all in the name of shaping better behaviour, but what we're really doing is trying to quieten our own discomfort.

Dr Lapointe invites us to pause right there. To look beneath the behaviour and ask what's happening in the child's nervous system. Because a child who feels safe will behave differently from a child who feels lost, frightened, or disconnected. It's not about raising "well-behaved" kids; it's about helping their nervous systems develop the way they're meant to—which, when you think about it, is a far better goal than compliance.

Of course, the same applies to us. The more I've paid attention to what's going on inside my children, the more I've had to face what's going on inside me. Beneath my own reactions, there's usually something softer waiting to be noticed. Parenting seems to be one long invitation to regulate ourselves so our kids can learn how to do it too.

I've come to see that we all move through three general states. There are the protective moments, when everything feels tight and reactive. Then come the learning moments, when space opens up and curiosity returns. And finally, the connected moments, when we feel safe enough to soften and listen again.

None of these states is wrong. Protection is the body doing its job, learning is the bridge back home, and connection is what we reach for once safety is restored.

These days, when I feel my jaw lock or my breath go shallow, I know I'm slipping into protection mode. I try not to judge it. I just notice. When my child erupts and I feel the pull to match his chaos, I pause and ask myself, *What's really happening here: fear, fatigue, or something unnamed that just wants a little care?*

Calm, I've learned, is contagious. Slow your voice, lower your tone, and nine times out of ten, they'll meet you there. It's almost unfair how well it works. (Although I have been known to take it too far, where my "calm voice" can wander into patronising territory. To anyone who's experienced that, my apologies. I'm aware and improving.)

There are a few other things I wish I'd learned earlier—they would have saved both me and my children a good deal of unnecessary tension...

Tantrums aren't misbehaviour.

Let's start with a radical thought. What if tantrums aren't bad behaviour at all?

What if they're just communication minus the vocabulary? Unless your toddler arrived with an emotional dictionary tucked under their chubby little arm, they're not plotting your downfall. They're just *feeling* wildly, honestly, and at full volume.

Most of the time, what we're seeing isn't disobedience but a system saying, *I don't know how to hold this.* Fight, flight, or full-body collapse next to Coco Pops. I've been there too, maybe not on the floor, but definitely close.

When I began to see tantrums as signals, not sins, everything softened. I stopped trying to win the moment and started listening to what it was trying to tell me. That's where the connection begins.

"Calm down" doesn't teach calm.

It might buy you a moment of quiet, but it doesn't solve anything. It's like slamming the lid on a boiling pot; the bubbles don't disappear, they just wait for a gap to explode through.

Calm can't be ordered from above; it has to be offered from within. Our children borrow our nervous systems until theirs are strong enough to steady themselves. When we meet their chaos with tension, they borrow that too.

I've muttered "calm down" through clenched teeth often enough to know I'm still learning. But I've also seen the benefits of not silencing and showing them that they are safe, even in the middle of the storm.

Emotional regulation is learned.

We've already established that none of the emotional work comes preloaded. It comes through learning, understanding, failing, and trying again. They're going to fall apart, just like they once did when learning to walk, only now it's their feelings stumbling. And just like walking, they don't improve by being scolded for falling; they improve by being supported.

I've already opened my heart to you about how badly I handled Muffingate. There were plenty of reasons, but the simplest was a gap in my skill, not in my intent. I didn't yet understand why I reacted the way I did, or how to do it differently. I wanted to get it right; I just didn't know how.

Our children are no different. They'll do better when they can. With enough practice, they learn that big feelings aren't dangerous or wrong; they're simply signs of something that needs care. And it's our response to those signals that teaches them how to grow.

Respect teaches understanding.

Toddlers need to feel our respect. When we kneel down, say their name, and really see them, we're saying with our eyes what words cannot always manage: *You matter.*

When children are met that way, they start to believe it. They learn that they're safe to be fully themselves, even when it's messy. Often, that learning comes from watching us, how we speak to the cashier, how we react when someone cuts us off, and how we handle being wrong. Those tiny, unfiltered moments teach them far more about being human than any lecture on kindness ever could.

When I stop, even for a second, in the middle of the chaos and meet my child's eyes, it's not simply about calming the moment. It's a way of saying, *I see you. You're safe with me.* That kind of seeing changes everything.

Presence builds safety.

Present parents build security. Sometimes that means muttering under your breath before catching yourself and softening your tone. Sometimes it's apologising after you've snapped or pausing when every part of you wants to do the opposite.

What our children remember isn't how often we stayed calm but how frequently we returned and worked at repair. We want to teach them that love doesn't vanish when things get messy. It bends, repairs, and keeps growing. Presence is about really being there and reminding them that they're not too complicated to be loved.

The world will teach them soon enough that mistakes have consequences. Our job is to show them something different.

Let them be who they are.

A few years ago, I read *Untamed* by Glennon Doyle. Not every page landed, but one part made a big impact. She wrote about her daughter Tish and how she used to try to make her more "pleasant" or "manageable." Then she stopped. "I quit trying to make Tish happy or pleasant and decided just to help her be Tish." Wow. We're not here to sculpt our kids into easier versions of themselves. Our job is to help them become more of who they already are, even when who they are is loud, stubborn, or completely undone over a muffin.

Josh wasn't being unreasonable that day; he was trying to explain himself in all his Josh-ness, someone who expresses emotional frustration loudly and with passion. Matthew, whom you'll meet later, expresses his with calm consideration. Who's right? Neither. They both have their strengths.

When I think about it now, I see how often I tried to make Josh more palatable. The real work was never to tame him, but to embrace all of him. He is a unique individual with so much strength and passion. Why would I ever want to change that?

Muffingate taught me that getting it right was never really the point. What matters is showing up, again and again, even when you'd rather not. Parenting isn't about perfect responses; it's about the small, human ones, a bit of patience, a softer tone, and the courage to start over when yesterday didn't go to plan.

Some days I manage it. Other days I don't. The difference now is that I notice. I celebrate the moments I get it right, and when I don't, I don't spiral. I just try again. That's what holding it lightly means—less judgement, more grace.

Our children won't remember every time we lost it. They'll remember that we came back for them. That's what stays.

Now that the lessons have had time to sink in, maybe it's time to look at the small, real-life things that make showing up a little easier.

TOOLS FOR EMOTIONAL GROWTH

Let's be honest: when I say tools, I'm not talking about a shiny set of parenting tricks that guarantee instant calm and children who tidy up without being asked. If those existed, I'd have ordered them years ago and handed them out at the school gate. What I'm talking about are strategies that will help you stay steady when life tilts sideways. This isn't about getting it right every time; it's about noticing what helps, trying again when it doesn't, and finding small ways to grow right in the middle of the mess.

Tool 1: The Toddler Feelings Wheel

I first used the Feelings Wheel in my coaching work to help adults who, like most of us, could name anger or happiness but not much in between. The wheel gives language to that in-between, the feelings we sense but can't quite name.

The same approach works with toddlers. A few colours, a few faces, and a few clear words are enough: yellow with a big grin for happy, red with a scowl for angry, and green with a soft smile for calm. It's not exactly a work of art, but it's an emotional map that even the smallest human can point to when words are still forming. It won't stop every meltdown (let's not aim for miracles), but it can turn chaos into communication, one little face at a time.

If I'd had the Feelings Wheel during Muffingate, I think I might have crouched down and said, "Josh, can you show me which face feels like you right now?" He probably would have jabbed the frustrated one with all the righteous fury of a toddler who'd been denied baked goods. And I could have said, "That makes sense. Waiting is hard, especially when you helped make something and can't have it yet." Would that have fixed it? Probably not. But it might have helped him feel understood, and isn't that what we're all really after?

Toddlers will still lose it over the wrong-coloured cup, and we'll still lose it right along with them. What the wheel offers is a shared language for what's happening beneath the surface. Instead of feelings being something to hush or control, they become something we can name together, even if it's clumsy or half-right to start with.

What I didn't expect was how naming his feelings made me notice my own and what I was carrying in that moment. Same tool, same learning.

And here's what using this tool might look like...

During a calm moment.

Try introducing the Feelings Wheel as part of play, not as part of problem-solving. That's when their curiosity (and yours) is wide open.

Long after Muffingate, I finally gave it a go. Josh and I were sitting on the carpet, laughing as he clomped around in his dad's shoes like a miniature accountant on casual Friday. The Feelings Wheel was blue-tacked to his door, bright and slightly over-designed.

I picked it up and said, "How do you think I'm feeling right now?" Without hesitation, he pointed to the happy face. "You're right," I said. "It makes me happy when you're happy too." It sounds small, but it showed him that faces tell stories, and those stories matter.

Then I teased, "And you? I think you're feeling..." and pointed dramatically to the scared face. He burst out laughing and jabbed the happy one with a grin. I added a few silly words like "goofy" and "bonkers" and watched him dissolve into giggles. He thought it was a game, which was precisely the point. Toddlers learn best through connection that feels safe and light.

Later that week, after a long day of "I do it myself!" negotiations, he curled up in my lap, ready for bed. I sighed. "I'm feeling tired tonight," I said. When he looked up at me, I said, "Can you find the tired face on the wheel?" He found it instantly. "That's the one," I said. "Just like me." Then I pulled an exaggerated grumpy face. "Sometimes when I'm tired, I get grumpy. Maybe it's better if I tell you instead of snapping." He nodded like a tiny therapist. "Maybe we can both use the wheel for that."

And that was enough. It wasn't about sleep or even about feelings, really. It was about showing that figuring them out together is always better than pretending they don't exist.

In the middle of a meltdown.

At school, we had two levels of maths: Standard Grade for people like me and Higher Grade for the geniuses who actually enjoyed algebra. What I've shared so far is the easy version of toddler emotions, the kind you can handle with a calm voice. But parenting doesn't stay easy for long. Suddenly, you're in the advanced exam with no calculator and far too many variables. That's when the big feelings hit, and the Feelings Wheel? It starts to feel like a joke. *Really? You want me to pull out a chart now?*

That's the moment you throw logic out the window and reach for the unexpected, because sometimes, the only way through the chaos is sideways with humour, silliness, or a bit of playful nonsense that reminds everyone this isn't a battle; it's a moment.

This is when I do exactly the opposite of what's expected. Cue humour. If I'd just said, "Whoa, that muffin is causing a lot of drama today," it might have taken the edge off. Or maybe if I'd turned it into a game: "Josh, did that muffin just shout, 'EAT ME NOW OR ELSE!'" Ridiculous, I know. But toddlers live for the ridiculous. They thrive on daft voices, pretend outrage, and anything that makes you look slightly unhinged.

I've even tried throwing my own tantrum right alongside his. He didn't flinch. Just looked at me like, *Make yourself at home, Mom.* No lesson learned there, and I didn't try it again.

But honestly, we're allowed to get creative in these moments. This isn't about giving in or negotiating with a tiny dictator; it's about recognising that sometimes, in the heat of toddler chaos, logic just doesn't land. So, think outside the box. You make the rules. If a silly voice, a dance, or pretending the muffin has feelings keeps everyone from imploding, that's good parenting in my book.

At bedtime or after the storm.

Have you ever seen those films where bedtime looks like a wellness advert: the parent reads three pages, the child yawns sweetly, whispers, "Goodnight, Mommy," and drifts off to dreamland? Honestly, who writes this stuff? People who don't have kids, or those with full-time nannies since birth, would be my guess.

Bedtime in my house was a contact sport. We'd have missing teddies, thirst emergencies, and the nightly encore of "just one more story." By the end, I'd be the one looking for my teddy and a glass of ~~water~~ wine. Still, on the rare night it all comes together, it's so perfect it almost makes me forget the 364 that didn't. Almost.

That's when I sometimes bring the Feelings Wheel back in. Nothing complicated, just a small, "Today was such a fun day. I feel happy. Goodnight, happy face;" or "Today didn't feel quite right. I was tired and a bit grumpy. Goodnight, grumpy face. Let's hope tomorrow feels better." Sometimes we even revisit the harder moments: "Remember how cross you were when I said, 'No'? Let's find that face and say goodnight to him too."

That's all it takes: a soft tone, a safe moment, and a name for the feeling. And while they're busy saying goodnight to their emotions, you might find yourself saying goodnight to yours as well.

Tool 2: Signing Feelings

I like the idea of using signing for feelings. A few simple gestures for happy, sad, angry, tired, or scared could have saved me a lot of detective work in the toddler years.

Picture this: your toddler's lip starts to wobble, but instead of a full-blown meltdown, they rub their cheek for tired or trace pretend tears down their face for sad. You mirror it back and say, "Yes, you're sad. I'm here." The drama might still unfold, but at least you both know what's happening. Sometimes that's all you need.

It also slows you down. When your child shows you a sign, it's a cue to pause instead of panic. You stop trying to fix the feeling and just meet them in it, which feels oddly revolutionary for something that involves hand gestures and a lot of guessing.

If you want to make it fun, turn it into a game. Draw a few faces on cards and take turns acting them out. Play "pick a face" at the dinner table or during a rainy afternoon. Toddlers love the silliness of it, and you'll love finally knowing what that face actually means. It's emotional education in disguise, which, frankly, is the only kind that works with toddlers.

If they come up with their own signs, even better. The goal is to give something to hold onto when their words haven't arrived yet.

Tool 3: The Problem Scale

I came across something recently called the "Problem Scale," and it really caught my attention.

It looks a bit like a giant thermometer, split into five colours:

1. Red (5): an emergency, the full siren, all systems go
2. Orange (4): a big problem

3. Yellow (3): a medium problem
4. Green (2): a small problem
5. Grey (1): no problem at all

What I love about this is that it helps our kids (and us) notice that not every problem is a crisis. Some things are just uncomfortable or annoying, and that's okay.

One version I saw had a dog next to the scale, teaching kids that the dog only needs to bark if the problem is a three or higher. I like the principle, but you could use any playful analogy. For example:

1. A fire alarm that only rings for orange and red problems, not every little spark.
2. A volume knob where the sound only needs to go up high for the really big stuff.
3. A traffic light: green for go (we can handle it calmly), yellow for pause (let's use our words), red for stop (okay, this one needs big help).

The main idea is that problems one through two don't need the alarm. That's where we practise using "wise words," phrases that bring us back to calm:

1. *This is hard, but I can do hard things.*
2. *I don't like this, but I can get through it.*
3. *I'm learning, and that means I'll get better.*
4. *I feel upset, but I can still make a good choice.*

For a three (medium problem), we practise slowing down and finding words instead of screams. That helps bring the "volume" back down into the safe zone.

For four or five, when emotions can feel scary or too much, it gives them a way to point them out.

In simple terms, for little ones:

1. Tiny problems → take a breath.
2. Medium problems → use your words.
3. Big problems → ask for help.
4. Emergency → it's okay to cry or shout.

This scale really teaches that emotions are *messages, not monsters*. It doesn't remove any of their feelings; it just helps them see the difference between the everyday bumps and the big emergencies. When kids see it laid out visually, it gives them a safe framework for practising handling their feelings in ways that keep both of you more balanced.

Tool 4: … and Breathe

Let's talk about breathing. Nothing groundbreaking, I know, but it works. Slow breathing tells your body, *It's fine, you're safe, and stop pretending you're being chased by a bear.* Your heart rate drops, the shoulders stop trying to become earrings, and the brain finally pauses long enough to think straight again.

Why save that kind of magic for adults in meltdown mode? Toddlers can learn it too. They don't need mindfulness apps or zen playlists, just a bit of playful logic: "Smell the flower" (inhale) … "blow out the candle" (exhale). Inhale, exhale, reset.

Of course, when a toddler is at Defcon 1, my calm little "let's breathe" suggestion probably wouldn't make a blind bit of difference, and that's fine. The point is to keep offering it until it becomes familiar. One day, it won't simply be something you do *for* them; it'll be something they reach for themselves.

The key: we are not powerless. There are tools available to help us manage our feelings, as well as those of our developing toddler, and they're worth keeping close. But more than that, it's about realising that these years don't have to be written off as the "hard stage" we must survive. They are challenging, but they also hold the possibility of something deeply worthwhile, even in the mess.

So, let me ask you: are you just surviving the days and bracing yourself for the next unpredictable storm, or are you willing to try something different? If you do, everything you hope to teach them in the years ahead will come more easily. The groundwork you're laying now is what builds the emotional fluency they'll carry long after the toddler years have passed.

FREQUENTLY ASKED QUESTIONS

Even after the muffins are swept up, the Feelings Wheel is back on the door, and everyone's mostly calmed down, questions may linger. Let's talk through some of the bigger ones.

Q1. What if my toddler's only response is "no" (to absolutely everything)?

That's okay. The goal isn't to get the "right" emotional label on the first try. It's to offer language and model awareness and to stay connected. Even if your child shrugs or shouts, they're still absorbing the intention behind your words. You could try, "It seems like you might be feeling mad or sad. Does that sound right?" They might not respond, but the seed is planted.

Q2. What if my toddler throws the Feelings Wheel across the room?

Ah, that's a bit trickier. Just because you introduce a tool doesn't mean they'll take to it straight away. That's not failure; it's feedback. Maybe they weren't ready, or maybe you weren't. Stick with it. Some days they'll poke at it; other days they'll ignore it completely. Either way, it's there when they need it, and so are you.

Q3. What if I completely lose it and say things I regret?

We all have moments we wish we could rewind, and times when the words came out sharp. That doesn't undo everything or disqualify you from being a good parent. It invites you to repair. "Mom got cross. I didn't mean to. I'm sorry. Can we have a cuddle and try again?" Or "I shouted when I was upset. I'm sorry."

There's a lot of power in those two little words: "I'm sorry." What our kids learn is that connection doesn't come from being perfect, but from repairing when things go wrong and proving that love and trust grow in the moments that follow the blow-ups.

Q4. How do I get my partner or family on board with this approach?

Not everyone needs to become a Feelings Wheel convert overnight. Emotional awareness takes time to develop, and it may show up differently for each person. Start by sharing what you're trying and why it matters to you. Frame it as something that helps everyone feel more understood, not just your toddler. Even if they remain sceptical, your modelling will begin to shift the family's tone. That matters.

Q5. What happens when this doesn't work at all?

Sometimes, despite your best efforts, the meltdown keeps going, the wheel flops, your calm voice disappears, or you're left standing in a puddle of feelings (most of them yours).

Remember that you are not trying to solve every meltdown. You're creating an emotionally safe space, and that takes time. Even when your child doesn't respond, their nervous system registers your presence. That's powerful, even if it's invisible.

Q6. Isn't this too advanced for toddlers?

You might wonder if a three-year-old can really describe how they feel. My answer? Absolutely. We underestimate young children all the time, forgetting that these are the same toddlers who memorise songs, mimic everything we do, and absorb language faster than we can keep up. Their brains are built for learning, and emotions are no exception. If we can teach them words like "cat" and "dog" without a second thought, why not "frustrated" or "disappointed" too? They learn what we show them, and that's where it begins.

Q7. When will I see results?

The short answer? Slowly. At first, you might see tiny changes: a pause before a scream, a little more eye contact, or a whispered "I'm sad" instead of a crash to the floor. These micro-moments matter. They're signs of learning. Be consistent in your approach. One day, in the middle of an ordinary meltdown, your child will name a feeling out loud... and your heart might just melt.

Q8. What if my child has meltdowns over everything?

Then you're in excellent company. Some children feel things with the volume turned up high, and it can seem as though every moment has the potential to explode. That doesn't mean you're doing anything wrong or that they're not learning. It just means their system is wired for intensity. It's less about eliminating meltdowns altogether and more about helping your child recover faster and begin to recognise what's happening inside them.

ESPECIALLY FOR YOU

If you're knee-deep in the toddler trenches, I already know a few things about you. You're tired, trying, and wondering how a person so small can hold so many emotions.

They're stretching their emotional muscles, learning how to exist in the world without falling apart, and they're doing it using your energy supply. That's no small thing when you're also holding a home, a job, and possibly other tiny humans together. As mothers, we patch up tantrums, referee sibling wars, and whisper, "It's just a phase" like a prayer, but we rarely raise a hand and say, "Help. I'm empty."

And that's where it all starts to unravel, when we pretend that we're fine. Because let's be honest, we're often not. When we can't admit it, Dragon Mom steps in. She's the self-appointed co-parent who storms into the kitchen, barking orders and breathing fire, convinced she's saving the day.

I know her well and have hosted her often enough to know she likes attention. I once made a sign that said, "Beware: Dragon Mom is visiting." The kids added tinsel and flashing lights, a not-so-subtle warning for all to take cover. But, behind the glitter and lights, it was really just me trying to say, *I'm not okay.*

The truth is, Dragon Mom isn't the enemy. She's what happens when you ignore the signs of what's really happening inside. Your work is to bring what's unconscious into awareness, so you have more choice about how you respond, not as the fire-breathing version of yourself, but as the one who's kind and understanding of her own limits.

With that in mind, let me say this as a fellow mother who knows how hard it is to keep showing up with an empty tank: your role isn't just to invest in your children; it's to invest in yourself, too. You're not just raising a child or three; you're raising yourself, learning, unlearning, and growing right alongside them.

So, love yourself the way you love them. Rest when you need to. Cry if you must. And if no one's said it to you lately, let me be the one who does. You are doing enough, even on the days it doesn't feel like it. Be gentle with yourself, the way you'd be with your child on a hard day. Let this version of you sit down, breathe, and be enough, because she already is.

FINAL THOUGHTS

Before I became a parent, I had a very clear vision of the calm and connected mother I was going to be. I pictured myself listening deeply, speaking gently, and never once losing my temper. In my head, I was practically the David Attenborough of parenting. "Here we see the mother," the voice would whisper softly, "effortlessly attuned to her child's emotional landscape."

As it turns out, parenting is not narrated, nor is it softened by a gentle lens. It is loud, messy, wonderfully unfiltered, exhausting, and hilarious, often all at once.

I don't carry Muffingate as a failure anymore. I carry it with gratitude because of what I have learned. Josh is seventeen now, perfectly capable of making his own muffins, and more than happy to tell me to wait, which makes me smile.

When I think back to that day, I used to believe the lesson was about patience and teaching him to wait his turn. That wasn't the case at all. It was about him learning to be little, and me learning to be big.

What we now understand from the science of child development is that children aren't meant to behave like miniature adults. They're wired for growth. Our role is to see them through the lens of development, not morality. We can't, by downward extension, take the expectations we'll eventually have of them as adults and apply them now.

When your child is having a meltdown, what they need most is connection, compassion, and empathy. They need an invitation for all that messy stuff to come out because whatever stays in will come out later—just louder, harder, and more complicated.

Every time we offer calm and connection in the middle of the storm, we're helping their brain learn what it means to self-regulate. We're doing on the outside what their nervous system will eventually learn to do on the inside.

And so, when we know better, we do better. For me, that knowing started with slowing down enough to notice what was happening inside, not just around me; realising that emotional connection isn't built in the calm moments, but in the messy ones, the ones that ask us to stay, repair, and begin again.

One day, you'll look back on your own moments that go completely off script, where the parenting manual fails, and all that's left is you, a small human, and a lot of feelings. You'll remember how it felt to get it wrong, and how, somehow, you both made it through.

Or maybe you'll be the woman in the supermarket car park, watching a young mother as her toddler flings ice cream across the tarmac. You'll see her face, that mix of disbelief and despair, and you'll smile, not because it's funny, but because you know. You've been there. You'll want to walk over, place a hand on her arm, and say, "You're doing fine. This too shall pass."

And when the next Muffingate comes, and it will, take a breath. Remember that every tantrum, every misstep, and every *not my finest hour* is just another chapter in the story of learning to love and be loved, as we really are.

Parenting doesn't shape us through the easy days. It shapes us in the waiting, the repairing, the trying again. One muffin, one meltdown, one perfectly imperfect moment at a time.

THE SKIM LOVER'S GUIDE

If you've landed here, life is probably full. Maybe small humans are climbing on you, or your mental load has hit capacity, and anything longer than a shopping list feels impossible. Think of this section as a quick reminder, a small anchor to return to when things settle, not the whole chapter, but a glimpse of what it's about.

In navigating your toddler's emotions, remember...

You are not alone.

Every parent has a Muffingate, the moment when it all goes sideways, emotions erupt, and you question everything.

Toddlers feel big and express loudly.

Their brains are under construction. Their feelings are real, and their words are still catching up.

You don't need a perfect plan.

You need presence. A breath. A pause. Maybe a Feelings Wheel. Something small to bridge the gap.

The magic is in the repair.

You will sometimes lose it, and that's okay. It's not the end. It's the doorway back to connection. "I'm sorry" is powerful. It counts.

Grace is not optional.

It's essential for them as well as for you. Especially for you.

You're growing too.

Moments like Muffingate don't break you. They build something in you that is softer, stronger, and more aware.

THE TAKEAWAY:

You don't have to get it right every time; you just have to keep showing up, even when your hands are full, even when your voice is tired, and even when the linen cupboard looks like a very tempting place to live.

Connection doesn't need perfection, just a moment of presence, right when it counts.

Part III

Navigating School-Aged Emotions

THE HEART OF THE SCHOOL-AGED CHILD

There's something about this stage of parenting that I wish I'd noticed more. You come out of the fog of nappies, broken sleep, and getting lost (that's Oxford Street coming back to haunt me), and suddenly there's this person standing in front of you. A real person, who can hold a conversation, make you laugh, and even tell you when your outfit is questionable. I don't think I really took in that shift from sheer survival to something that actually felt like friendship. It's like stepping off the rollercoaster for the first time in years and realising, *Oh right, this is what solid ground feels like.*

When I talk about "school-aged children," I mean those pre-teen years, the sweet spot between cuddly chaos and full-blown attitude. Although to call it a sweet spot is slightly misleading, because a lot is going on under the surface, where we are once again required to shift how we parent. It's that tuning again, to what's being said and how, when it's not being said and why. We may have survived the toddler meltdowns and taught them a few basics about feelings, but honestly, there's still a long way to go.

This is the stage where they still want you, but only on certain terms. One day, they'll lean in for a kiss at the school gate, and two days later, you'll get the hand signal that says, *Absolutely not.* They'll beg for a sleepover, then hand you a list of rules about staying upstairs and pretending you don't exist. It's funny, until it's not, because that's when you realise that they are inching away from you and learning to be their own person. Which is precisely what they're supposed to do.

My daughter marked her first venture into this kind of independence by setting my oven on fire, simply because she saw herself as grown-up enough to do it solo. I wasn't quite ready, but I recognised the importance of the moment and hovered from a nearby room. Thankfully, it was only the oven repairman I had to call, not 999.

This new trial-and-error phase is how they grow. They can be fearless explorers one moment and suddenly hesitant about walking into a class without a familiar face. They can glow with pride when the teacher gives them a gold star, and then fall apart when the opposing football team scores a goal.

Josh is a prime example. A foul or unfair goal could bring an emotional collapse for the entire world to see. We tried reasoning, calming, and even threatening, but nothing worked. In the end, the only option was to let him ride it out while we pretended to be wildly interested in the match behind us, cheering on whoever's kid happened to have the ball as if he were our own. Was this a strategy for dealing with overwhelming emotion? You bet. Was it foolproof? Hardly. But unless you're a Year 4 boy, you'll never fully grasp the injustice of a dodgy foul or the sheer tragedy of a disallowed goal.

And yet, for all the drama, there are still the tender reminders they're not as big as they think. A small hand reaching for yours on the way to school, or a quick glance from that same football sideline just to check you're watching. Those are the moments we treasure.

I could name a hundred emotionally charged moments from this stage of parenting, but one of the toughest was the season a teaching assistant had to peel my howling son off my legs just to get him through the classroom door. Every morning, I'd stand out of sight by the bicycle rack, listening to his sobs while the teacher gently reminded him that I'd be back later. I'm still not sure who carried more emotion in those moments. If I had to guess, I'd say me, because while he was soon distracted by friends and football, I was the one making the long, grief-filled walk home, trying to look like a functioning adult.

For a friend of mine, it looked different. She had a newborn and was already bone-tired, but her middle child insisted on dragging a mattress into her room every night so she could sleep beside her. Sweet in theory, but in practise, it was challenging. Between the broken nights, endless negotiations, and the sheer weight of being needed by everyone at once, she was running on empty. It wasn't disobedience. It was a child saying, *I need you*, without having the words for it.

And then there are the smaller, quieter signals, the ones that are easy to miss if you're not paying attention. One of my children (no names mentioned) had a habit of eyeing up everyone's portions and quietly claiming the biggest one. It drove me crazy, because I didn't understand the message behind the action and didn't think to push for more. What that child really needed was help uncovering the feeling beneath the behaviour. If I could go back, the gift I would have given her wasn't another exasperated sigh or lecture on fairness. It would have been curiosity. I'd have sat beside her and said, "Tell me what's really happening here."

There's always a reason; it just doesn't always come with words. Even now, I wonder what that sense of *not having enough* really meant for her. What fear was sitting underneath it? I don't know, because it never occurred to me to ask. Instead, I corrected the surface behaviour and created a whole lot of unnecessary mother frustration that could have been avoided if I'd just given her credit for being a human with needs, rather than a child who didn't have any.

During this school-going age, a child's needs, emotions, whatever you want to call them, spill out into the world and get tangled up with other children. That's new, when it stops being about what happens under your roof and starts showing up in the playground, the classroom, and the lunch queue.

Growth now becomes about adaptation, testing where they belong and finding their place in a world that suddenly feels much bigger than family. A good day can hinge entirely on who they sat with at lunch or who saved them a place in line, and it doesn't take much to tip the scales. Sometimes it's not even about what's said, but the smallest phrase delivered at just the right (or wrong) moment.

When mine were young, the ultimate playground threat wasn't clever or complicated; it was, "You're not coming to my party." Six words with astonishing power. At that age, being invited to a party is the social equivalent of having your name up in lights. It's proof that you belong. So, when someone says, "You're not coming," it's not just about missing cake and balloons; it's about being pushed outside the circle. It's astonishing how young children are when they start to understand the currency of belonging, and how cruel it feels to be cut off from it.

I'll never forget the first time I heard one of mine say it. I froze. Surely not my gentle, big-hearted child. But there it was, a declaration of exclusion, and a tiny rehearsal for the way the world sometimes works.

They're older now, and I've reclaimed that phrase for my own purposes. If one of them is dragging their feet about something, I'll throw out a cheerful, "Fine, then you can't come to my party." They roll their eyes, sling an arm around me, and say, "Okay, Mom, point made." Progress, of a sort.

While there's humour in that memory, friendships are also where some of the deepest bruises form. Suddenly, being liked matters more than being picked for the football team or whatever the playground's version of fame happens to be that week. The questions start to change, too. It's no longer, "Are you proud of me?" but, "What will they think if I mess it up?" Not, "I feel left out," but, "Why didn't they choose me?" ... "What's wrong with me?"

You want to protect them from it all, of course you do, but part of you knows that this is exactly where the learning happens. These moments are their practice runs for the bigger stuff that's coming. The best we can do is stay nearby while they figure it out. Be the person who says, "This hurts, doesn't it? I get it."

Early in my parenting journey, I came across Dr Ross Greene, a clinical psychologist who instantly made me feel better about not having all the answers. His take was simple: stop leaping in to fix everything. Just collaborate. Listen. Which, okay, I realise sounds dangerously close to Vanilla Ice. *Stop, collaborate and listen. Ice is back with a ...* Honestly, it could be our new parenting anthem. Our job isn't to swoop in with solutions; it's to help them figure things out with us, to problem-solve together rather than turning them into problems to be solved. Revolutionary, really.

I wish I could say it's that simple. It isn't. Parenting at this stage feels less like following a manual and more like detective work. It's easy to forget that the same child who can dress themselves, finish homework, or strut off the pitch like David Beckham is still only learning the language of emotions. I had to remind myself of this often, paying attention to the sharp words over dinner, the diary that suddenly became off-limits, or the tummy ache that always arrived on a Monday morning. Even the quiet, "I don't want to talk about it," was usually code for, *Actually, this really needs talking about.*

The story that follows might look like your run-of-the-mill playground drama, but for me, it was anything but. It was my daughter, Michaela, trying to make sense of the heartbreak of being left out. My instinct was to swoop in and fix it, because that's what we do; instead, I sat with her in it. I let her feel it, even when it nearly broke me.

When I look back now, I see that the gift of that season wasn't the pain, but what grew from it, and while the story that follows focuses on Michaela and a particular friendship wobble, I hope you'll see that the tools inside it don't belong to any one age or stage. They're the same tools we can use whether we're parenting a six-year-old, a teenager, or even trying to make sense of our own grown-up friendship tangles. These moments don't have to be wasted. They can become the ground where resilience takes root, where our children learn that their feelings matter, and where we learn that presence is enough.

NO LONGER ON THE GUEST LIST

While the world was bracing for the Millennium Bug and stockpiling tinned food, I was packing a hospital bag, preparing to meet our newborn son. At least, that's what I thought. This wasn't the result of neighbourly predictions about how I was carrying, or an old wives' tale about the shape of my bump. It came from an earlier scan, when the midwife casually announced, "He's growing beautifully," before carrying on as if nothing unusual had been said. I remember blinking, thinking, *He? Did she just say 'he'?*

Neil and I had planned to keep the sex of our baby a mystery until delivery day, so that statement was like someone wandering into the cinema midway and blurting out the ending, except my "film" still had nine months to run, and now I knew how it ended. Still, I chose not to spoil the surprise for Neil and carried on as if nothing had changed. But of course, it had. You can't unknow the sex of your baby once it's been said. It changes how you imagine them.

For the remainder of the pregnancy, I quietly bonded with my growing son, taking the opportunity to lay some important ground rules. "Sweetheart, if sport is your thing, I support you 100%. Football, swimming, tiddlywinks, whatever you choose. Just please, not rugby." I couldn't bear the idea of my baby being flattened by a wall of teen testosterone in studded boots, and I figured that I had about six months to gently make my case.

By mid-September, I was as ready as I'd ever be. My hospital bag was packed with a blue-and-white outfit, a matching hat, and, tucked at the bottom, a miniature plastic golf club, a subtle nod to the ceremonial gender reveal, while also quietly declaring, golf, yes… rugby, never.

You can imagine my surprise when, after seventeen hours of persistent labour, "he" turned out to be a "she," swaddled in blue, with a plastic golf club accessory. I was delighted at the turn of events. We returned home with what I was convinced was the most beautiful baby born that morning, despite her cone-shaped head and the forceps indentation stamped like a souvenir across her cheek.

From the beginning, Michaela had a quiet magnetism and a presence that drew people to her. Adults softened around her, and children followed her lead without even realising they were. She was fiercely loyal, sharply articulate, and delightfully opinionated. Definitely the child you wanted in your corner, but also the one you thought twice about debating unless you came well prepared. It's no surprise that Michaela now works in law, carrying the same boldness to challenge, question, and hold her ground as she did when she was a child.

That mix of confidence, intensity, and quick wit was always both Michaela's superpower and her Achilles' heel. She wasn't rude, just wonderfully direct, and in those early years, that boldness rarely caused too much trouble. Even so, I carried a small, unspoken relief when Michaela found her way into a close-knit group of girls. There was something deeply reassuring about seeing her wrapped in the safety of inside jokes and whispered secrets, part of a circle that gave her the kind of belonging every parent hopes their child will find.

They called themselves the Fabulous Five, with regular sleepovers, playdates, and a string of "shows" performed in our garage, lounge, or patio. Costumes, microphones, and dramatic intros were always part of the package, and we were obliged to watch every performance. The storylines were usually paper-thin, with no real climax to speak of, but we still applauded, begging for encores, as if we'd just witnessed the next West End hit.

The thing about friendships is that as children grow older, the rules begin to change. What once felt open and spontaneous slowly became more selective, and I could sense the shift beginning with Michaela. At first, it was subtle, a slightly cooler tone when certain names were mentioned, and a lack of enthusiasm about invitations that once would have thrilled her. They were the kinds of details only a parent notices. Because I knew what it felt like to be on the edge of belonging, I watched carefully.

I told myself I wasn't hovering or interfering; still, I couldn't shake the quiet dread that the day might come when Michaela's strong personality, the very thing I admired most about her, would begin to clash with the unspoken rules of social survival.

So, I did what any slightly anxious, overly involved mother might do: I tried to stay ahead of it. If I could host the playdates, make the snacks, and be the "fun mom" (without tipping into embarrassing territory), maybe I could keep her in the mix. I wasn't trying to control her friendships—not really. I just wanted to build enough warmth and safety around her that being left out wouldn't have anywhere to land. Deep down, I knew that even the strongest kids can crumble a little when the invitations dry up. Just because Michaela could argue her point better than most adults didn't mean she was immune to the sting of exclusion.

To counteract the possibility, I played Sharpay. I made brownies. I clapped through every single garage performance, even the ones where the microphones didn't work and nobody remembered their lines. I wasn't chasing some gold-star mother status; I was just desperate for her to belong. Is that so wrong?

Most afternoons, they'd tumble out of school in a noisy, joyful pack. You could hear them before you saw them: chattering, laughing, deciding whose house had the best snacks or the comfiest sofa. But on this day, Michaela walked out alone, clutching her jumper as if it were a lifeline. Her eyes stayed fixed on the ground, her steps heavy and slow. I could see the rest of the gang in the distance, arms linked and beaming. Completely intact. Without her.

My stomach dropped. I didn't need an explanation, as the scene told me everything. If you've ever seen your child on the outside of a friendship, you know exactly what I mean. The pain is written in a way that needs no explanation.

She climbed into the car without a word. She didn't look at me or do the half-smile thing she normally did when she was upset but was trying to be okay. She just pulled the door shut, wrapped her arms tight to her chest, and stared straight ahead.

At first, I said nothing, hands on the steering wheel, ready to go but not turning the key.

"I don't know what happened," she said, her voice small. "Actually... I do. I just, ugh, I don't know." Her eyes flicked toward the windows, scanning the world outside to ensure no one was coming. I waited. "They didn't keep a place for me at lunch today," she finally said. "They just ... walked out together. All of them, like I wasn't part of them anymore."

She then continued, circling the truth with half-finished phrases and hesitant pauses, as if naming it would make it real. Her hands twisted in her lap, her voice shook, and the pain she was trying so hard to hide was etched across her face. I didn't get the whole story, not then, but the scattered pieces gave me enough. The Fabulous Five had become four, and Michaela was the one who'd been pushed aside.

My first response was one of pure outrage, that knee-jerk reaction when you see your child on the receiving end of something they don't deserve.

"Maybe I did something wrong. Maybe I said something, or they want to be friends with someone else."

I turned toward her and opened my mouth, probably about to say something along the lines of "Well, did you ask them?" or "I'm sure it's just a misunderstanding."

The tears she'd clearly been trying to hold back began to trickle down her cheeks. This was real, raw pain that she'd probably held through lunch, the rest of her lessons, and all the way across the playground to the car.

My heart ached for her. It's hard to see your happy, bubbly child so crushed by something as simple and devastating as feeling like they don't belong.

As cruel as this scenario was, my rational mind told me that it all boiled down to a lack of maturity. Kids don't stop to think, *What will this do to the one we're leaving out?* They just don't. Not until someone teaches them, or until they've felt it themselves. Yet for the child left standing on the outside, it doesn't feel like immaturity at all; it feels like rejection, confusion, shame, and heartbreak, all new emotions to a growing child.

"You can't be my friend anymore" may be a simple phrase, but it cuts deep. For Michaela, this was her first time hearing it, even if the words themselves were never actually spoken.

I felt completely helpless, which is not a place I do well. What mother does? It's unbearable to watch your child hurting. Every part of you wants to step in and shield them from that pain. That's the mama bear in us. You wouldn't dream of going near a bear cub in the wild. The mother would be on you in seconds. We may not have claws or sharp teeth, but emotionally we're just the same. When our kids are hurting, the instinct is primal: protect, defend, rescue. The hard part is holding that instinct back, knowing that sometimes the most loving thing we can do isn't to jump in swinging, but to sit with them while they weather the storm. That connection is the key to emotional development.

I couldn't climb into the minds of those girls and undo it, and she didn't need my pep talks. What she needed was space to feel what she was feeling. For mothers, that's the part that nearly breaks us because sitting still while they sit in pain feels like doing nothing, but it isn't nothing. Sometimes it's the most important thing we can do.

Of course, this is the story I am telling you. In reality, it's easier said than done. The second any of mine are hurting, I reach for my glue, my tape, and sometimes even a magic wand. I was practically born with a roll of emotional duct tape in my hand, ready to patch, smooth, and tie it all up with a triumphant, *Voilà, problem solved!*

Stepping back didn't even cross my mind. Instead, I wracked my brain for solutions until one sprang to mind: *the teacher.* Of course. Who better? Teachers know everything: playground politics, who's in, who's out, and why your child is suddenly eating lunch alone.

For a moment, I felt relief. Finally, a plan. And so, I blurted out, "But maybe we could... what if I just..."

"Mom, please," she whispered. "Let's just go."

Something in those three words stopped me in my tracks. I don't know if it was the quiet plea in her voice, the unspoken *not now*, or the courage it must have taken for her to even say it, but whatever it was, it cut through my rescue mission. It made me realise she wasn't asking me to fix it; she was asking me to stand with her in it.

One of the hardest lessons I've had to learn, both as a coach and as a mother, is that fixing isn't the same as helping. Fixing is me patching together a solution that makes me feel better, but it doesn't give a child the chance to wrestle with their own feelings and find their own footing. As much as I love a quick fix, I've seen how much stronger kids become when they're given time, space, and gentle guidance instead of instant answers.

Which meant that dialling 999 to the teacher wasn't really an option. So, I swallowed every instinct, turned the key in the ignition, and drove us home. For a born fixer like me, that restraint deserved a medal.

Once we were back in the safety of our lounge and away from the car park stares, she finally let go. The tears came in a rush, then the words, spilling out in broken pieces. At first, she wasn't telling me what she felt; she was just telling me what had happened. That's when I realised how important it is for children to start with the facts, the sequence, and the who-said-what, because it gives them something solid to hold onto. It's like building the outer frame before you can fill in the middle. Once the story is laid out, the feelings can begin to take shape.

The trouble is, as mothers, we don't always handle this part very well. Without meaning to, we fall into one of two camps. One, we jump right in with, "She said WHAT? No, she didn't! Who does she think she is?" And suddenly the story is about our outrage instead of their hurt. Two, we skip ahead and start handing them labels: "So you must feel left out... maybe you're angry... maybe you're sad." In doing that, we quietly rob them of the chance to discover those feelings for themselves.

A better way is to let them tell it in their own words while we stay present. What they need most is space, which is hard when every part of you wants to tidy it up. This is the gift of gentle listening. It has a way of saying, *I'm here. Take your time.*

That's exactly what I tried to do with Michaela. I let her piece it together at her own pace and fill in the little details she only noticed as she said them aloud. I didn't rush her into naming feelings because I trusted they would surface in their own time. She was able to talk openly without interruption, and I was able to see her exhale into that freedom.

After a few minutes, she said, without looking at me, "I know I'm not easy. Like... I can be intense, and I talk a lot, and sometimes I don't know when to stop." This raw insight wasn't something I was expecting, and while there was a measure of truth in what she was saying, I could also feel that there was a risk of it sliding into self-blame. "Michaela," I said gently, "this doesn't mean there's something wrong with you." She wiped her face roughly with her sleeve. "It kind of feels like there is," she muttered. "Because why else would they all just... drop me?"

I wanted to argue with that thought, tell her how amazing she is, how cruel people can be, and that this will pass, but I knew none of that would land right. She wasn't ready for reassurance. She needed company in the pit.

"You don't have to make sense of it right now. You don't even have to explain it to me. I'm just... here," I said lovingly. She nodded and then replied, "I didn't want to go to school this morning. I just had this feeling. Like, something was off, but I went anyway, and now I wish I hadn't." Then, barely audible: "I don't want to go tomorrow either."

I put my hand on her leg. "Okay," I said. "Let's talk about tomorrow when we get to tomorrow."

Silence again. Then, barely above a breath: "Mom, I don't understand. What did I do wrong? I hate them and I don't want to see them ever again."

"That's hurt, love," I said, choosing not to focus on the word "hate." Children can be quick with words like that, and it's tempting to want to call them out on it. "We don't hate people," or "don't talk like that." But those words are simply a shield. What's underneath is sadness, confusion, and, if we're not careful, we start parenting the surface emotion instead of staying present with the pain under-neath. So, I didn't correct her. I didn't try to talk her out of it. I just sat there, knowing this was the part where she needed someone to see the hurt, not silence it.

In the days that followed, her feelings began to rise, one by one. I could see the sadness sitting there, just beneath the surface, waiting to be felt. But every time it came close, she'd retreat into anger, because anger is louder and easier to hold than heartbreak. But most of the real work happened behind her closed door, where I'd hear those deep, heart-broken sobs, the kind that punch straight through you, and every instinct demands you go in and fix it. But I didn't. I sat outside and let her have her space, knowing that this is what growing up looks like: pulling back and trying to work it out on her own. Of course, knowing doesn't make it any easier to watch.

Sadly, exclusion like this is rarely a single moment. She had to walk back into the same classroom day after day, face the same laughter, the same whispers, and the same invisible wall that kept her on the outside. It was another reminder that her place had shifted. She saw it in the empty chair beside her, the party she didn't know about, and the group chat she wasn't added to. That's brutal. At eleven years of age, "You don't belong here anymore" doesn't just sting. It shakes your foundation.

What made the entire situation that much more difficult was how the parents seemed to fall in line with their children's behaviour, as if they'd all signed up to the same unspoken pact. How does a group of friends fracture so visibly, and not one adult says a word? To this day, I'm still baffled by it. It was as if a silent memo had gone out: *She's out. Act accordingly.* No one said anything, not to Michaela and not to me. Just silence, cool and deliberate.

I wanted to shake the mothers and ask if they'd all collectively lost the plot. In my head, I even drafted a PowerPoint: *How Not to Act Like a Twelve-Year-Old When You're Forty.* I pictured myself standing on the school steps, shouting, "Well then, you can't come to my party!" And honestly, that might have been the most satisfying thing I could have done. But I didn't. Instead, I swallowed it down and reminded myself that this wasn't about me. I didn't need to win points, prove a statement, or, worst of all, make a scene. What I needed was to stay exactly where I was:

alongside my broken-hearted daughter, helping her untangle what her feelings were really trying to tell her.

It's a strange kind of heartbreak, sitting beside your child while they learn the hard truth that people can be unkind, and that sometimes, the grown-ups aren't much better. But there's also something quietly powerful about watching them begin to find their way through it. The tears, the silence, and the anger all have a purpose, and it's through that process that Michaela began to make sense of herself.

If we can hold back from fixing, meddling, or tidying it all away, we get to witness something far more beautiful: our child beginning to make sense of their own heart. You can almost see the moment they find a small bit of language for the big feeling, and the load lifts, just slightly.

While this book isn't about coaching, I can't ignore how much of what I learned there shows up in parenting. My own journey started with a desperate urge to help others unlock what was stuck inside them, probably because I'd spent so many years locked out of myself. I'd built these invisible walls without even realising it, and they kept me from a lot of good things. What I've learned since is that most of us already have what we need. We just need someone patient enough to sit with us while we find it.

Coaching gave me someone to walk beside me, and that's what I tried to do for Michaela. I sat next to her and let her talk until the noise settled, until she could start to see what she already knew deep down. In coaching, we call it "holding space"; really, it's just love without the urge to rush in and rearrange everything. When you get it right, you can almost feel the shift, that moment they realise the strength was there all along. That's where the courage starts to grow.

I tried to help Michaela name the things she couldn't quite say out loud, so she could see that none of it made her broken. They were feelings, not facts. They didn't mean she didn't belong or that she had to become someone else just to be chosen again. The hurt at that age can whisper, *It's your fault, you're too much, and you will never belong.* If we don't help them unpick those lies, they start to believe them. And that, more than any schoolyard drama, is what leaves the lasting mark.

As we sat there together, I leaned in and offered her the words she couldn't quite find.

"Maybe it feels like everyone saw what happened and nobody cared."

"Maybe you're scared this feeling will never go away."

"Maybe it feels safer to pull back than risk being hurt again."

I wasn't telling her how she felt. I was just laying out a few gentle guesses, like open hands, so she could take what was hers and leave the rest.

After a while, her words started to make more sense to her. She told me how humiliating it felt to walk past them in the corridor, how exhausting it was to pretend she didn't care, and how scary it was to think it might always feel this way. It wasn't the whole story, but it was enough. Once those feelings had names, they weren't just swirling around like fog anymore. They became something she could start to understand.

As for the ending? Well, it wasn't the kind you read about in children's books. The Fabulous Five didn't have a big reunion; there were no "best friends forever" hugs, and her spark didn't come roaring back overnight. What came instead was a steady confidence that hadn't been there before—not the loud, look-at-me kind, but the quiet knowing that comes from walking through something hard and realising that you not only survived but were stronger because of it.

We kept talking long after the drama itself had faded. We talked about anger, rejection, jealousy, betrayal—all of it. We didn't rush past the uncomfortable bits. We held each one up and asked, "What's this feeling trying to tell us? Is it useful? What should we do with it?" Sometimes the answer was clear; sometimes it wasn't, but saying it out loud mattered, and naming it gave it a way out.

Michaela started to see that feelings don't have to be hidden, nor do they have to explode. They can be explored in silence or out loud. She learned that anger was okay if she paused long enough to ask what it was really about. We did that together, like emotional detectives, holding each feeling up to the light and asking, "Will this help, or will it hurt more?" Most of the time, the answer was no, but that didn't matter. The naming was enough.

It wasn't an easy chapter for either of us, but it was an important one, and it deserves to be seen for what it was: a story of her growth and mine. She learned she could walk through pain and not fall apart. She could name it, speak it, and still stand tall on the other side. I learned that my child was far more capable than I'd ever given her credit for. I saw it in how she grew through that moment, and I've seen it since. Every time life throws something new at her, that quiet strength reappears, like it's been waiting all along.

Moments like these don't come with fanfare or clear-cut endings. Most of the progress happens quietly. That's what makes the next chapter so special. It's about those small, steady victories you almost miss because when the next hard thing comes (and it always does), it helps to remember what you've already learned, how far you've already come, and that you've done hard things before.

THE QUIET WINS

Progress in parenting doesn't always look like progress. It isn't shiny or obvious or something you can tick off a list. Most of the time, it's the sort of growth that sneaks in while you're just getting on with life. Still, I'm convinced we should celebrate it more. We're so quick to name frustration and guilt, but we rarely name joy or pride. And that's a shame because those emotions are worth teaching our kids to recognise too.

The trouble is that our brains are a bit Eeyore by nature. If he'd been narrating the Fab Five fallout, it might have sounded something like: "Well, I knew that friendship circle wouldn't last. Yes, I made it through, and Kanga was kind enough, but it'll only happen again. It always does. Nothing ever really changes." You can almost hear the sigh, can't you? That's the Eeyore in all of us, the voice that skips right past the growth and heads straight for the next disappointment.

But wins are so important to hold onto. When we focus on what went right rather than the drama that caused the growth in the first place, we give ourselves a gift. In noticing the wins, we build up a little internal storehouse of reminders: we've been through hard things before and came out the other side—we can do it again.

Some wins are smaller.

I remember those evenings when the kids were little. Bedtime was a battlefield of teeth brushed at snail's pace, pyjamas that somehow disappeared every single night, and the nightly negotiation over the final sip of water that was apparently vital for survival. Most evenings, by the time I got everyone under their duvets, I was emotionally, spiritually, and physically done.

With Michaela, bedtime often felt less like winding down and more like gearing up for Round Two, mostly because of three small words. "I love you." They should have been the sweetest words of the day, but when you've been up since five a.m. and your patience is hanging by a thread, even love can feel like a challenge.

"I love you."

"Love you too."

"To the moon and back."

"A gazillion times."

"And then up the Eiffel Tower."

"Up to the Tower and back."

"Up to the tower and back and then to Jesus." (Because he always felt the furthest.)

But one night was different. Everything just… flowed. No shouting, no bribing, no tears, and just the right amount of "I love yous" to make everyone feel, well, loved. When I closed their bedroom doors, the house was still, and for the first time all day, so was I. Whether I recognised it at the time or not, that was a small win.

Other wins are big.

Months after the friendship drama, one of the Fabulous Five (or should I say Four?) mothers, whose life I had graciously spared, rang me out of the blue. She told me how amazed she was at the way Michaela had carried herself, and how graciously she'd handled such a painful situation. Then came the part I didn't expect. "I'm sorry," she said. "At the time, I didn't see the damage this situation caused."

It wasn't a grand, public apology, or a dramatic handshake. Just a quiet moment that said a lot. It told me that the strength Michaela had built behind closed doors had somehow made its way out into the world. Her private work hadn't just held her together; it had shifted something in someone else, proof that when we practise something in private, it really can ripple outward.

More than that, it showed Michaela that understanding and expressing her emotions didn't make her fragile; it made her strong in a way that actually lasts. She didn't just survive this experience; she grew through it, and without even realising it at the time, so did I.

Needless to say, I could easily list all the things Michaela did well, but I chalked up a few wins of my own when I managed to...

Stay in the moment.

It sounds simple, but for me, staying in the moment is anything but. My instinct is to fix, tidy, or find the plan and make it all make sense. Sitting still while someone I love is in pain feels like being trapped in a room with no doors. I can't breathe, but I know if I open my mouth, I'll ruin everything.

So, I sat there, basically wrestling with myself. I kept thinking, *Don't jump in, don't rescue, don't wrap it up too* neatly. Because fixing it too soon would have buried it, and I knew that would only teach her that pain is something to avoid, not something to understand.

When we shut up long enough to listen, our kids start to find their own words. They realise pain isn't proof that they've failed at life; it's just part of it. Our job is to guide them through it and help them build the language that makes it a bit easier to understand. Children can survive not being happy; they really can. But it's so much easier when we're willing to sit with them in it.

Make room for all the feelings.

That moment stretched both of us, but it also brought us closer. Michaela learned that she could bring me every version of her feelings, even the messy, unfair ones that came out like character assassinations or half-baked stories. And

I learned to let her, because really, what good would correcting her do? They were her feelings, not mine to edit.

I've learned that the accuracy of the information doesn't matter nearly as much as the honesty. When we correct our children mid-feeling, they don't hear, *You're wrong*; they hear, *This part of you isn't welcome*. I never want to be the reason my child hides what hurts.

Emotions don't always tell the truth about the world. Still, they always tell the truth about the heart, and when a child realises their feelings are safe with you, they start to understand themselves better. Giving Michaela that space was my way of saying, *You can bring it all here, and I'll still be here when the dust settles.*

That's what it means to hold space. It's not silent agreement or perfect listening. It's just love that stays put while the storm passes.

Let her find her own way.

The biggest win for me was stepping back and letting Michaela figure it out for herself. Do you know how hard that is when you're running on caffeine and nerves? Every part of me wanted to jump in and say, "Here's the plan, do this, job done," because that's quicker. You fix the thing, pat yourself on the back, and everyone can go back to pretending life is under control. Except that's not really learning. That's me running quality control on her life, and mine.

Instead, I tried something new. Rather than throw her a ready-made solution, I asked a few questions: "What do you feel? What do you think should happen next? What matters most here?" I know we've touched on similar questions before, but I hope you can see the thread; they're the same ones we once asked ourselves, and not far off the ones we used with our toddlers. The words change, but the heart of it stays the same.

Sometimes Michaela had the answers. Sometimes she didn't. And sometimes she went round in circles until we both wanted to scream. It was hers to wrestle with, not mine to fix.

When I finally stopped to listen, I realised she didn't need me to lead. She just needed to know I believed she could do it, and she did. She carried herself through it with courage that still amazes me today. She might have come out a little bruised, but those marks have long since faded. What we remember now isn't the hurt; it's how much we both grew. What a beautiful way to remember something that once felt impossible.

It took me years to understand the importance of slowing down to notice the wins. Just like emotions, they need to be named or else they slip quietly into the background. The good news is that they don't have to be elaborate. "That made me happy." It can be just enough to connect the win with the feeling, so they start to see that what they do makes a difference.

WHAT STILL STRETCHED ME

As much as I've talked about the wins, I'd be lying if I didn't also admit to the struggles. Nothing about this came naturally. I wasn't gliding through it with the calm curiosity and gentle wisdom I now aspire to. I was biting my tongue, second-guessing, and practically sitting on my hands to stop myself from trying to fix it.

This is where *presence over perfection* sounds lovely in theory, but in practice, it's a long, uncomfortable, and often emotionally inconvenient stretch. Learning the language of emotions, understanding them and how to process them isn't instinctive; it's something you grow into, one messy and meaningful moment at a time.

My struggles included …

Resisting the rescue mission.

As you know, I had to override every fixer instinct in my body. Watching Michaela in pain was agony. Even while I was nodding, breathing, and doing my best impression of a grounded, emotionally attuned parent, my brain was rehearsing emails to teachers, messages to mothers, and even imaginary speeches that, thankfully, never saw the light of day.

What stopped me wasn't a great well of wisdom. It was Michaela's quiet voice: "Mom, let's just go." At the time, it felt like defeat. Now I see it differently. Maybe that was her version of sitting with what she couldn't explain and letting the ache exist without trying to patch it or push it away. I didn't recognise it then, but I do now.

Patience with my children's raw emotions is still a muscle I'm stretching. It doesn't grow by reading more books or perfecting the right script. It grows in the quiet spaces where I resist fixing, where I stay when leaving would be easier, and where I witness the storm without trying to control the weather.

Making doubt take the back seat.

I've always had a soft spot for the underdog, and oddly enough, when my own child is hurting, the "other side" sometimes feels like the one I need to defend. My instinct is to zoom out, balance the scales, and ask: *What's the full story? Maybe she misread something or overreacted or was partly to blame.*

On paper, that sounds fair, but in practice, it doesn't give the assurance that feelings are worth validating, and that's what Michaela needed most. Yet, I felt the pull to dissect her story and scan for what she might have done wrong. This sort of cross-examination would have chipped at her trust.

This is where patterns really start to matter, because they sneak into our parenting whether we notice or not. I'll give my mother a respectful nod here. Whenever I showed a hint of sadness or anger as a kid, she'd go full Pollyanna on me. If you don't know Pollyanna, she's that relentlessly cheerful orphan from the book of the same name, the one who could find something to be glad about in absolutely everything. My mother was basically her in human form.

Her intentions were good; I know that now. She was trying to make things better by lifting me out of whatever I was feeling. But looking back, I see it as another form of fixing. Instead of, "I hear you, that sounds hard," I got, "Well, at least…" or, "Look on the bright side." It sounded kind in theory, but in practice, it meant sitting alone with the bits that didn't feel bright at all.

With Michaela, my version wasn't Pollyanna; it was a full emotional audit. I'd analyse, weigh, dissect, and turn every feeling into a research project, and only once I'd figured out the "right" response would I let myself feel anything. It was exhausting. I lost connection by prioritising analysis over empathy.

I catch myself doing it to this day, but I'm learning. I try to pause before I dive into problem-solving, to listen first and let trust take the lead. It's slower, but it feels a whole lot more human.

Looping, loud, and still unfinished.

Michaela's a processor, just like me. Sounds ideal, doesn't it? Two deep thinkers, calmly unpacking life together. In reality, it nearly finished me off.

She went over the friendship fallout again and again, like a detective on a never-ending case: who said what, who didn't, and who stood there. I wanted to stop her. To say, "Okay, love. We've been through this. Let's move on." Then, when it became the only topic of conversation, I wanted to yell, "Enough already! We've covered every scene in full technicolour with bonus commentary, can we pleeeaaase just roll the credits?"

But I had to keep reminding myself that she wasn't being dramatic; she was doing the slow, painful work of trying to make sense of her pain. Looping, revisiting, and rehashing were all part of her healing. Feelings don't tidy themselves away in order. They come back messy and loud until they feel seen.

It reminded me of the endless bedtime repeats of, "I love you." The coming back again and again, just to make sure the love was still there. That's what this was too—a way of checking: *Am I safe; are you still here?*

My stretch was remembering that this wasn't about efficiency. It wasn't about getting to the end of the conversation or finding closure. It was about showing up, even when I was done and she wasn't.

Talking about feelings doesn't come easily to everyone. It's awkward and raw, and sometimes it hurts more before it helps, but there are gentle and practical ways that make it less about fixing and more about staying. Those are the ones I'll share next.

TOOLS FOR EMOTIONAL GROWTH

When I first brought out the Feelings Wheel back in the Muffingate years, it was about 50% connection and 50% survival. Joshua needed help figuring out what on earth was going on inside him, and honestly, so did I.

Over time, I've realised that most of the so-called "tools for kids" should really come with a label that says, "For parents, too." Half of my biggest "aha" moments have come from trying something I thought was purely for their emotional development, only to quietly think, *Oh, right. This is for me as well.*

The beauty of emotional growth is that it is a *we* thing, not just a *you* thing. It's messy and mutual. We're not just teaching our kids how to handle their feelings; we're in the thick of it with them, fumbling, learning, getting it wrong, and showing them that you never really graduate from this stuff.

So don't think of the tools that follow as something to hand down like a manual. Think of them as invitations, little openings to get curious together.

Tool 1: The Feelings Wheel

For toddlers, we used the Feelings Wheel as a simple way to name big, messy feelings. What I didn't realise then was that this brightly coloured circle of feelings would keep turning up through every stage, just with new layers. Here, it's less about identifying the basics and more about refining, like a map that helps us go beyond, "I feel bad," into something more precise: "I feel overlooked," "I feel hesitant," or "I feel exposed."

This matters because the clearer the words, the clearer the picture. "I'm sad" might get a sympathetic nod, but "I feel left out" is a story. It tells us what the sadness is really about. When we know the "why" behind the feeling, we can respond in a way that actually meets the need. "Sad" is vague. "Left out" is specific, and specificity invites empathy.

Think about it. If your child says they're sad, you might try to cheer them up. But if they say they feel left out, you're more likely to sit beside them and acknowledge the ache of not belonging. That's connection. When our kids feel truly seen, not just managed, they learn that their emotions carry meaning, not shame.

In the long run, our children will grow into adults who can navigate conflict better, regulate more effectively, and form stronger relationships. They're not left guessing at their own inner world because they now know how to read it and share it.

When the friendship fallout with Michaela began, she didn't storm through the door and say, "I feel rejected." She didn't have that language yet. What I got instead was a thud, her backpack hitting the floor, and a quiet, "I don't want to talk about it." In that moment, handing her the Feelings Wheel would've been like tossing a drowning person a textbook. But later, when the worst of it had passed, it became a gentle way in.

Instead of asking the dreaded, "Are you okay?" (which always got me a very convincing "I'm fine"), I'd say, "Do any of these words feel close to what's going on inside?" That's when "sad" became "left out, invisible, not enough, confused, lonely, ashamed." Words that finally gave us something to work with.

It's worth mentioning that while Michaela was thoughtfully circling her feelings, I was mentally scanning the wheel for the fiercest synonym for "livid." Honestly, the thing could've used a whole extra section: "How mothers feel about other mothers who make everything worse."

The Feelings Wheel won't fix everything, but it does give us a starting point, and something that makes it easier to stay in the discomfort together.

Tool 2: The Mood Meter

It may sound like something you'd find in a therapist's office next to a Himalayan salt lamp, but the Mood Meter is actually quite brilliant. Created by the Yale Centre for Emotional Intelligence, it's simply a square divided into four coloured boxes:

1. Red = high energy, unpleasant (angry, anxious)
2. Yellow = high energy, pleasant (excited, inspired)
3. Blue = low energy, unpleasant (sad, tired)
4. Green = low energy, pleasant (calm, content)

That's it. You can draw it on the back of an envelope and ask, "Which colour are you in today?" or "What shifted you from one to another?"

It sounds too simple to work, but that's precisely why it does. Once you get used to naming how you feel, you start catching yourself sooner. I've definitely muttered, "Red quadrant. RED QUADRANT," while stuck in London traffic behind someone who has apparently decided rush hour is the perfect time to learn to drive. Just saying it out loud buys me enough of a pause to not lose my mind completely.

I used it a lot during the *High School Musical* friendship saga. Before the school run, I'd take a beat and ask myself, "Okay, where am I on the grid?" If I was already glowing red before we'd even left the driveway, it didn't take a Yale professor to know the morning wasn't going to end well. But if I could shift myself into green, even just a little, Michaela stood a better chance of getting the calm version of me, not the sharp-edged one.

At pickup time, I'd watch her crossing the playground. *Backpack slung loosely?* Probably blue. *Storming toward the car?* Full red. *Avoiding eye contact?* Some new colour not yet invented, but you get the idea. It wasn't about diagnosing her mood; it was about me noticing, so I could meet her where she was instead of dragging her into where I was. (Tuck that thought away, because in the next part of the book, we'll dig deeper into how the state we're in matters and why tools like this are just as much for us as they are for our kids.)

What I love about the Mood Meter is that it gives you shorthand for the emotional chaos. None of us wants a five-step emotional plan before breakfast. Sometimes all you need is a colour. Michaela could say, "I'm red today. I need space," and that was enough. No probing. No fixing. Just honesty and a bit of grace.

Speaking of which, I wish I could say, "I'm magenta today, I need a holiday," and everyone would just nod and hand me a boarding pass. But I digress...

Wouldn't it be something if we all had a shared language? Honest naming and the grace to let each other sit with it without fixing, rushing, or judging. That, to me, is the heart of emotional connection.

Tool 3: The "What's Up?" Prompt

In his book *The Explosive Child*, Dr Ross Greene suggests starting with something as simple as: "What's up?" instead of diving straight into a lecture or a full-blown TED Talk on behaviour.

When I first read that, I actually laughed. *What's up?— really? Can the same two words I'd use to greet the postman make a difference?* Turns out, they can.

When I tried it, I realised how powerful it was. Instead of "Why are you acting like this?" or "What on earth is wrong with you?" a door opened and offered a safe space to go deeper.

"What's up?" doesn't demand an explanation or force a child into confessing. It's not confrontational. It's curious. It gives them the chance to put into words (or at least try to) what's going on inside. Sometimes the answer was a shoulder shrug or a grumble that sounded nothing like progress. Still, other times, it was the key that unlocked what they hadn't been able to say: "I feel left out;" "It's not fair;" "I don't know why, I just feel off."

The beauty of this prompt is that it doesn't fix the problem there and then, and that's the point. It slows you down and reminds you to listen first. It tells your child, *Your feelings are safe here.* Over time, it builds trust.

It's such a small shift, but one that changes the whole atmosphere. Instead of shutting them down, it opens them up. Instead of making them feel alone in their struggle, it tells them they don't have to carry it by themselves. It gently teaches that naming what's going on inside is the first step to finding a way through.

Tool 4: Hug the Raw

This one isn't technically a tool you'll find in a parenting book, but it's been as useful to me as any chart or grid.

Years ago, I listened to a teaching by Tsoknyi Rinpoche, a Tibetan monk, whose gentle, almost tender way of meeting emotions caught my attention. He didn't analyse them, fix them, or try to rise above them. He simply welcomed them, as if even the messy, uncomfortable ones deserved a seat at the table.

That struck me because it was the opposite of everything I'd been taught to do with difficult feelings. My instinct was to push past them, tidy them up, or dress them in something more acceptable before letting them out in public. His approach was different. He said three words I've never forgotten: "Hug the raw."

He spoke about the feelings we usually push aside: sadness, shame, fear, and that gnawing sense of not being enough. He called them "beautiful monsters." Not because they're easy to love, but because they're part of us.

That flipped something in me. I'd spent years trying to tidy up my emotions or at least make them look presentable before showing them to anyone. He was saying the opposite: stop fixing and stop judging, just sit with them. Be kind to the mess.

What if, instead of bracing against our most complex emotions (ours or our children's), we got curious? What if we stayed long enough to hear what they were really trying to tell us, beneath the tantrum, the silence, or the slammed door? That's what he meant by hugging the raw; it's saying, *It's okay. I see you. I'm not going anywhere.*

Isn't that what we all long for? To have our hardest moments witnessed with gentleness, where our presence says that we don't need to be anything other than what we are right now.

Parenting has taught me that emotions aren't mistakes to fix; they're messages trying to get through. The kindest thing we can do, for ourselves and for our kids, is to sit next to them and listen, to stop trying to tidy them up and just be there until they shift on their own, because they always do, eventually.

If you find yourself in a raw moment, maybe you can remind yourself to sit with the feeling and give it a gentle hug.

FREQUENTLY ASKED QUESTIONS

Q1. What if my child won't open up about their feelings?

That's normal. Kids at this age are basically emotional oysters. Everything important is tucked away inside, and the more you pry, the tighter they clamp shut. It's not defiance; it's just them figuring out who they are without you hovering with a flashlight.

Instead of launching into, "What's wrong?" (which, let's face it, usually gets you a grunt or a slammed door), try something softer, like, "You don't have to talk about it now, but I'm here when you're ready." It takes the pressure off.

Q2. My child says they're "fine" when they're not. What should I do with that?

"Fine" is the classic shutdown. We've all used it. I still do when someone asks how I am, and I can't be bothered to unpack the emotional carnage of my day. It's no wonder our kids learn it too.

The trick is not to pounce. If you go straight in with, "You don't *seem* fine," they'll dig their heels in. Instead, try gentle curiosity. Something like, "Okay, you say you're fine, but your face looks a bit heavy today." Or even, "If fine had a colour, which one would it be?"

You're not prying; you're just leaving the door ajar. The point isn't to get the full download there and then; it's to show them that you've noticed, that you care, and that when they're ready to step through that door, you'll still be on the other side.

Q3. How do I help my child name emotions when they don't yet have the words?

Start with you. Honestly, the best way to teach emotional language is to speak it yourself. Say things like, "I felt a bit overlooked today when I didn't get invited," or "I'm grumpy because the washing machine just ate another sock." It normalises feelings and shows that words for them actually exist.

Tools like the Feelings Wheel can help too, especially if you make it a bit of fun. Ask, "What's the weirdest word on this thing?" or "Can you find a word for how you feel when your maths teacher announces surprise homework?" You're sneaking in emotional literacy under the guise of play.

The lovely bit is, the more you explore together, the more fluent they become, not because you've drilled it into them, but because feelings start to sound like something everyone's allowed to talk about.

Q4. What should I do when my child keeps bringing up the same issue repeatedly?

This is where I practise my own life-saving breathing exercises because patience is not exactly my spiritual gift. Looping is processing, not drama. It's the brain's way of circling something until it starts to make sense. They're not stuck on repeat to annoy you; they're doing the slow, messy work of healing.

That said, presence doesn't mean being endlessly on call. It means showing up meaningfully, not martyring yourself. If your tank's empty, it's okay to say so; the magic is in *how* you say it. Try something like, "I really want to listen to this properly. Can we talk after I've had a minute to catch my breath?"

By giving a clear *when*, you're not brushing them off; you're letting them know they still matter, and that you'll come back to it when you can really listen. That reassurance builds security, not dismissal. Almost without them realising, it teaches that connection is about two people's needs being respected, not just one.

Q5. What if I feel more emotional than my child does?

You're not the only one, and it doesn't mean you're doing it wrong. Sometimes we carry more intensity because we see the bigger picture and how this moment might ripple out. We also may be remembering our own past hurts, while our children are simply standing in the here and now, not yet sure what they feel.

It's okay to have feelings about their feelings (or lack of them). The goal isn't to shove yours down or pretend you're calm when you're clearly not. It's to hold them lightly, to notice what's happening inside without making your child responsible for it.

You can say something like, "I've got some big feelings coming up too, and I want to make sure I respond carefully, so I'm going to take a breath, and then I'll be right here with you."

That's emotional modelling at its best. You're not performing calm; you're practising it. You're showing them what it looks like to feel deeply and still stay in the room, and that's something they'll remember far longer than the moment itself.

Q6. How can I encourage emotional honesty without turning every moment into a "teachable moment"?

Ah, yes, the accidental life coach trap. I know it well. You ask one innocent question and suddenly you're knee-deep in a full-blown emotional workshop, while your child's eyes glaze over and they start planning their escape route.

The truth is, emotional honesty doesn't need a speech; it just needs space. Sit with the feeling; don't fix it. Sometimes the best thing you can do is shut up and nod. If they open up, try "That makes sense; I hadn't thought about it that way." Or just a quiet, "Yeah."

That's it. No lesson, no moral, just validation. Being seen and believed *is* the lesson.

Q7. How do I know if I'm doing this right?

If you're here, asking that question, you already are. The parents who worry about getting it right are usually the ones doing far better than they think.

This isn't about perfect words or polished wisdom. It's about the small, ordinary moments that whisper, *I see you.* The cup of tea left outside their door, the quiet drive home when neither of you says much, or the simple, "Do you want to talk, or just hang out?"

You don't have to have the answers. You just have to keep turning up, even when it's messy or awkward or silent.

ESPECIALLY FOR YOU

Please don't read this and think I've nailed emotional regulation, because honestly, I'm no different from anyone else trying to raise small humans without losing my mind. I've snapped, shouted, stormed off, and if I'm being completely honest, at least one of those things probably happened today.

None of this is about perfection. It never was. It's about intention. It's about wanting to connect, even when you don't get it right the first time or the tenth. If all you managed today was sitting next to your child while they cried, that's enough. If all you had to offer was a hug while swallowing your own tears, that's also enough. If all you could give was your presence, you guessed it... more than enough!

Recently, a client who was struggling to connect with her child said, "I am present. We eat dinner together, I drive him to school, and I ask about his day." I knew exactly what she meant. I used to think the same thing. *I was there, wasn't I? I was physically in the house, making food, folding laundry, keeping the show on the road. If that's not presence, then what is?*

But real presence isn't just being *there*; it's how you show we *see* them. It's looking up from the washing or the laptop when they walk into the room. It's pausing before offering advice, even though every cell in your body wants to. It's saying, "That sounds hard," without trying to make it easier. It's holding space for their silence, their sighs, their half-answers, and trusting that being there, quietly and consistently, is more powerful than any speech you could give. These little "touch points," as I call them, matter.

A friend once told me she lingers in the kitchen long before mealtimes, not because there's anything to cook, but because that's when her kids start hovering. She doesn't interrogate or look them in the eye. She just potters about, pretending to wipe already clean counters. They might not say a word, but they can feel her presence.

Similarly, Josh wasn't feeling well recently, somewhere between a cold and early onset man flu. Instead of fussing, I grabbed a coffee, lay on his bed, and pretended to scroll while he played guitar. It wasn't long before he said, "Mom, listen to this…" and just like that, connection happened. It reminded me that sometimes presence isn't doing or saying; it's simply being nearby.

If there's one thing I've learned, it's that our job as parents isn't to fix our children; it's to tend the environment. If the ground isn't safe, and connection, calm, and belonging are missing, then that's where the work needs to start.

Sometimes that means adjusting yourself, and sometimes it means adapting to the environment.

When your kids start to pull away, it's easy to take it personally, to feel like their independence is rejection. It's not. They're just figuring out who they are, and that's exactly what they're supposed to do. If you keep finding small ways to connect in those ordinary moments, the balance holds.

And while we're here, let's talk about being the "cool" mom—not in the sparkly, performative sense, but the kind of parent your child's friends actually want to be around. The one who knows when to appear with snacks, when to fade quietly into the background, and when to listen without turning into a human lie detector. So much of a child's emotional life happens in the pack, and if your home feels like a place where they can all exhale, you'll learn more than any heart-to-heart could ever reveal. You don't have to interrogate or perform; you just have to be there, warm, open, and not too cringe. (I've definitely crossed that line a few times, but the key is knowing when to retreat with dignity.)

The other gift in this is that it keeps you close, even as they start to pull away. A lot of their growing independence is about pushing us out, and that's natural. But being the safe adult in the background means you're still in the picture for your child and sometimes for their friends, too. Over the years, a few of my kids' friends have found their way to my kitchen table mid-meltdown, and I've offered them exactly what I've learned to offer my own: a calm presence and a place to be heard. I do it not just for them, but with the quiet hope that there are other moms out there doing the same for mine.

Our job is to hold that sense of belonging steady. No matter what storms blow through, our children need to know that they are safe with us, that they belong. That foundation becomes the template they'll carry into every other relationship for the rest of their lives. It's the soil in which resilience, courage, and connection grow.

So, from one mom to another, keep going. You're doing far better than you think.

FINAL THOUGHTS

There's something about this stage, this in-between place of not-quite-little and not-yet-grown, that asks us to shift gears, not just in how we parent, but in how we see.

We often find ourselves scanning for something specific: a clear cue, a direct need, or a simple solution. However, much of what unfolds in these years is foggy. Our children are beginning to notice more about themselves, others, and their place in the world, but they don't always know how to make sense of it. And truthfully, neither do we.

What we do have are small, imperfect, human moments that help us tune in. A story that sits differently, a sentence that stumbles out and tells you there's more underneath, and a pause that lasts a little too long. These are the moments that invite us to lean in, not to decode everything, but to simply be there when they're ready.

There was a time when my parenting focused on keeping my children happy, and why not? Who wants to see their child go through heartbreak and pain? Certainly not me.

But somewhere along the way, I realised that when we focus too much on happiness, we end up making our children afraid of everything else. Because what we're really saying, underneath the reassuring smiles and the "you'll be fine" pep talks, is I can't handle your sadness either.

And so, they learn that feelings such as sadness, anger, disappointment, and rejection—all the normal, necessary parts of being human—are somehow unsafe.

The irony, of course, is that when happiness becomes the goal, anxiety often becomes the outcome, because how do you live in a world that's full of change, loss, and imperfection if you've been taught that discomfort is a danger sign?

The real work is helping them build resilience instead. Resilience is being able to sit in the mess without rushing to sweep it up. It's knowing that sadness won't swallow you whole, that disappointment passes, and that you can feel the pain and still be okay.

Every time we meet our children's emotions with calm rather than panic, and with curiosity rather than correction, we're showing them what safety feels like. We're lending them our regulation until they can find their own.

I once read a quote from a brain surgeon who said that the most important skill a human being can learn, more than intelligence, more than charm, and more than multitasking, is emotional regulation. It's not about being endlessly happy; it's about being endlessly human. Everything I've read about emotional intelligence points back to the same thing: that emotional regulation is one of the most essential skills we can learn. It's the ability to feel something uncomfortable without immediately bolting for the exits.

The ability to feel something uncomfortable without immediately bolting for the exits. I love that. Because it's not about being endlessly happy; it's about being endlessly human.

And that, I think, is what this middle bit of parenting was really about—not smoothing the road, but walking alongside Michaela while she learned to handle the bumps.

In the end, it's not about knowing what to do; it's about staying open when nothing makes sense. It's holding space for their growing pains and your own, meeting the grey with gentleness, and choosing to show up, not as the perfect parent, but as the steady one.

FOR SKIM LOVERS

If you've landed here, you're not alone, and you're not cheating.

Whether you're skimming before school pickup, previewing what's ahead, or coming back to make sense of what you've just read, this is your shortcut to the heart of it. It's not the whole chapter, and for now, that may be enough.

When you're navigating the emotions of your school-aged child ...

You're not imagining it.

This age is full of big feelings and social shifts that can catch even the most prepared parents off guard. It's quieter than toddlerhood, but no less intense.

Not all pain is loud.

Sometimes it whispers through closed doors, tired eyes, or a backpack dropped just a bit too hard. Responding to the silence is as important as responding to the noise.

Fixing it isn't the answer.

And honestly, thank goodness. What your child needs most is someone steady, and someone who can stay, even when it's awkward and aching.

Presence is your real tool.

Not polished or performative. Just you, sitting beside them in the ache, holding space they didn't know they needed.

You will want to fix it.

Sometimes that feels easier. You'll imagine emails, phone calls, and justice served.

Breathe. Let that pass. Then sit back down beside your child.

Your belief is the balm.

More than advice. More than solutions. It's what heals.

It tells your child: *Your feelings are real. You're not over-reacting. You matter.*

Repetition isn't drama.

It's processing, and if they keep coming back to the same story, it's because they're trying to make sense of it. Let them.

Tools can help.

Try a Feelings Wheel, a Mood Meter, or a simple question like "what's up?" Use them gently, playfully, without pressure. They're not for fixing. They're for finding each other.

Grace is the golden thread.

For them, and for you. Especially when you're stretched, second-guessing, and craving emotional closure that may never come.

You're growing too.

This isn't just their story. It's yours too. Your own friendship wounds may echo. Old fears may stir. That's okay. You get to tend to those, too.

THE TAKEAWAY:

You don't need to have it all figured out. You don't need the perfect response or the flawless fix. In this tender, tangled season, what matters most is that you stay close, present, and steady.

What they'll remember isn't the advice or the solutions, but the way you stayed, the way you listened, and the way you let it be.

That's the legacy of presence: quiet, unpolished, and unforgettable.

Part IV

Navigating Teen Emotions

THE HEART OF A TEEN

Do you value your teen? Didn't see that one coming, did you?

When my kids hit adolescence, I wasn't thinking about value. I was just trying to survive their general teen-ness, which already felt like a full-time job. Looking back, maybe winging it wasn't the best plan because when the real battles began, I found myself knee-deep in the emotional version of *The Hunger Games*, just shrugging and hoping for the best.

Yet value is where it all begins. Not the "I love you no matter what" kind of value, but the kind that says, *I see you, even when you're slamming doors and rolling your eyes.* It's about recognising their worth before their behaviour improves and about remaining calm when they're testing every ounce of your patience. If we want to help them navigate their emotional world, we have to start by appreciating who they are right now, not who we hope they'll grow into someday.

And that's not easy. If I'd found a shortcut, I wouldn't be selling it or even loaning it out; I'd invite you to move in. We'd live together, drink tea, and I'd share every aspect until you'd cracked the code, but, as far as I can tell, there isn't one.

Adolescence has a reputation for a reason. I like to think of it as the Ibiza of parenting. Just hearing the word makes you brace yourself. You don't need to have been there to know the stories. Say "Ibiza," and you don't picture tranquil coves; you picture strobes, noise, chaos, and too little sleep. The same goes for teens. Mention the word, and parents who've been there nod knowingly, like veterans of a long, loud summer.

But maybe adolescence, like Ibiza, has more to it than its reputation. Beneath the glare and the noise, there's something alive and real and trying to make sense of itself. That's the contradiction, isn't it? All that chaos on the surface, and underneath, something tender and unsure, figuring out how to be in the world. And while it's messy and loud and exhausting and occasionally smells like Lynx Africa, parenting in this season asks us to stay open and curious right in the middle of all that push and pull.

Josh, who is no longer a muffin-throwing toddler but a fully-fledged adolescent, gave me a glimpse of that balance yesterday. Something had clearly upset him, but instead of talking, he disappeared into silence. In a chatty family, that kind of silence stands out. Every attempt to connect was met with slouched posture and one-word answers.

It's times like these I half-joke about googling teenager rehoming services, but since I'm already emotionally invested in this chapter, it felt hypocritical to check. So, I reached for my emotional first-aid kit of gentle questions: "Would you like to talk, Josh? Is something bothering you? Can you tell me how you are feeling?"

While this may sound like I had him reclining on the sofa while I played therapist, I wasn't. I subtly wove these questions into what we were already talking about. He shrugged, as expected, and said, "I don't know." Also expected. Third child round, I've learned not to take offence.

Half an hour later, my phone pinged. *I'm in bed and tired ... if you would like to say goodnight.* And there it was, the push and pull. It wasn't about bedtime. It was his way of saying, *I'm trying to be independent, but I still need you.*

That's the quiet middle ground between go away and don't leave me—and you don't want to miss it.

Now, let's take a step back and look at what's really going on under the hood of a teenager. On the outside, they look like adults-in-waiting, which can make it jolly confusing because we start treating them that way. But inside, it's emotional carnage. Hormones are raging, emotions are pulsing, and biology is basically shouting, *Welcome! It's time to test-drive independence,* whether they're ready or not.

For those who haven't reached this stage yet, let me save you the suspense: the journey toward independence often starts with a kind of parent replacement. They either act as if they've earned a PhD in everything or turn to their new guru, Dr Google.

Josh recently gave me a textbook example. At seventeen, he came down with a nasty case of diarrhoea. In full mother mode, I reached into my well-stocked get-well bag for the usual remedy, something that's been saving stomachs for generations. But Josh wasn't having it. Google had informed him that he shouldn't take it alongside his ADHD medication. I suppose I should give him some credit for at least thinking that part through.

Eventually, with him still attached to the loo, I phoned our local pharmacist and put them on speaker. The pharmacist confirmed exactly what I'd said and calmly assured Josh that my suggestion was perfectly safe. I'm fairly sure he thought I was either trying to kill him or that I'd ridden a dinosaur to school, which, in his mind, made my medical knowledge somewhere between outdated and extinct.

All of this is completely normal, or so I keep reminding myself. Their brains are basically under renovation, with the sensible part wrapped in dust sheets while the emotional control tower is running the whole show. Feelings arrive first, long before logic has even found its shoes. So no, they're not just moody for fun—they're living inside an intensity they don't yet know how to manage. It's exhausting for them, and honestly, for us too. The trick, I think, is remembering it's not a personal attack. It's just growth, loud and messy and completely human.

There's something else worth remembering. While they're working out what they feel, they have absolutely no interest in explaining it to us. It's like the moment they turn thirteen, someone unplugs half their vocabulary and replaces it with text talk: idk, smh, or a well-placed emoji. And this is going to shock precisely no one, but despite all the beautifully nuanced words on the Feelings Wheel, the one that rules the teenage years isn't even on it: "fine."

For heaven's sake, what does *fine* even mean? I've lost count of how many times my children have used it. "How was the maths exam?" Fine. "How do you feel about today's hockey win?" Fine. "You survived the zombie apocalypse, shaken at all?" Fine. I don't want fine. Give me anything else. Annoyed. Confused. Utterly betrayed because I made pasta instead of pizza. I can work with that. *Fine* is emotional tofu. It has no flavour, offers no substance, and leaves you hungry for more. Which is why I was delighted when I stumbled across its secret acronym: Feelings Inside, Not Expressed. I almost said, "I've got you, you little blighters," but decided to play it cool and make a mental note instead. Fine was no longer going to be the end of any conversation. My new, neat little tool would see to that.

The hard part is giving those feelings inside enough space to find their way out and turn into words that make sense. Which isn't easy because with teens, feelings usually show up long before language does. If we try to squash them or tidy them up too quickly, resistance shows up. They're not being defiant; it's just their teen wiring. *This is who I am. Let me figure it out.*

Maybe that's why the bedroom becomes their kingdom. What looks like isolation to us is really their chance to regroup. Our challenge is to remember that a closed door doesn't always mean *Go away*. Sometimes it means *I still want you near, just let me decide how near.* That distance can sting, but there's something about it that feels familiar, isn't there? Like my old hidey-hole. The only difference is that mine's more abstract, and I've just had more years to make it look functional. They haven't quite worked that part out yet.

I used to think my role was to tip the scale with rules and advice, but I've learned to make myself available in a way that says, *I'm here when you're ready… even if ready looks nothing like you'd expect.* At one point or another, all three of mine have phoned me from upstairs while I was sitting downstairs. Yes, phoned, from inside the same house, and not a mansion either. A London-sized house where you could shout from kitchen to bedroom without even needing to stand up properly. At first, I dismissed it as peak laziness. I mean, how heavy could their legs possibly be? But over time, I've come to see it as winning the parenting lottery. If they are dialling in from twelve steps away, it means something matters enough to break their silence. I drop whatever I'm doing and take the stairs two at a time, heart thumping at the rare chance of a conversation that might, just might, last longer than "I'm fine."

Now, for those of you getting a little excited by the prospect of actual communication, I should probably mention a small caveat. These invitations don't always unfold into anything remotely profound. More often, it's something deeply pressing like, "What's for dinner?" or "Can we get takeout?" Occasionally, if the universe is feeling generous, it's both. Still, it means something, doesn't it? Whether it's for chicken chow mein or something that actually matters, the connection is there, and it's enough to make me pick up the phone every time.

This season, we are the testing ground, the people they can bounce their emotions off of without losing their footing. To do that well, they need a safe place, plenty of space, and parents willing to do the work to help them get there. This brings me back to where we started: value.

When they feel genuinely valued for who they are right now, they start bringing more of themselves into the room simply because it feels safe to do so. Our words and actions need to say, *You matter enough for me to walk this with you, not fight you through it.* Then, even when their emotions get loud and messy, they know we're not going anywhere. To me, that feels like a far stronger foundation to build on than the wing-and-a-prayer approach I once thought would get us through the teen years.

So, if you're wondering what this part of the journey feels like, buckle up. This is my unfiltered version of growing with an adolescent. It's where you'll discover how that missing value piece showed up in real time and how I began turning those rough, raw parts of my parenting into something resembling growth.

And to tell it, I have to go back to when Michaela was a teen and how we learned to navigate the journey together.

WHY CAN'T YOU BE LIKE OTHER MOTHERS?

Michaela is back in the spotlight, my brave firstborn and chief test pilot of every theory I thought I understood about parenting a teen. As you know, I didn't have much of a plan, just this vague hope that I could shape-shift into whatever the moment needed. So, when Michaela marched into adolescence, tossed her bag in the corner, and declared, "Teen years, I've arrived. Let's see what we can unleash," I got the shock of my life. From the start, she was independent, articulate, and terrifyingly good at dismantling an argument. Her emotional range was vast and included enough eye rolls to power a small emoji factory.

At her best, her energy and humour wrapped us in laughter until our sides hurt. When the darker, *I'm not okay* side showed up, the rhythm of our family tilted, and we all found ourselves waiting to see which tide would roll in next.

The tricky thing about this stage is that young people look like they've got it all figured out. They project confidence, competence, and control, and Michaela did that perfectly. She ran her own social calendar, made decisions like a CEO, and spoke with the certainty of someone twice her age. It was so easy to forget that underneath all that polish was a brain still wiring itself together.

Of course, independence comes with a shadow side. Every teen has one. Michaela's sounded a lot like, *Help me, but don't expect me to like how you help.* She wanted me to know exactly what to do without her saying a word, then rejected it with enough force to knock me sideways.

It reminded me, in a strange sort of way, of Mary Howitt's *The Spider and the Fly*, where the fly drifts into the spider's parlour, completely unaware of what's waiting.

"Will you walk into my parlour?" said the spider to the fly;

'Tis the prettiest little parlour that ever you did spy."

I'm not saying teenagers are cunning spiders setting traps. It's more that, as parents, we sometimes end up as the fly, caught in a web we didn't see forming and tangled in both their and our expectations.

I think that's the real gap in parenting advice. It's not the sleepless nights or the toddler tantrums. We're warned about those. It's the years when they look grown but aren't yet built for the weight of it all. We leave the maternity ward with a newborn, a stack of leaflets, and a false sense of readiness. What's missing are the Terms and Conditions, something like...

Dear Parent,

Congratulations on your brand-new human. There will be no returns or exchanges, and certainly no upgrades.

As part of your discharge pack, we are required to inform you that while the "snuggle" and "I love you" functions will operate beautifully for the first twelve years, a self-installing software update known as Teen 2.0 will activate shortly thereafter. Features may include a sudden preference for one-word answers, high sensitivity to parental advice, and a relentless drive for independence. The occasional "always polite" edition exists but is rare and randomly assigned.

Please retain this notice for future reference. It will remind you that this isn't a manufacturing fault, just a standard feature of the model you received.

Best of luck,

Customer Care

Absurd little thought experiments like this have always helped keep me sane. They take the edge off what can feel like a long group project where one member insists on working alone and sighs dramatically when you ask how it's going. Still, there's truth in it. Teenagers are just trying to figure out how to be human, and they need us to stay close enough to remind them that all will be okay.

If I were writing a real parenting manual, one that didn't sugarcoat the mess, it would simply remind us to guide gently, hold steady, and stay curious.

I don't think Michaela ever meant to make life complicated, but somehow, she did. The straight line of life was more of a rough guideline to her. She'd drift, bump, wobble, steady herself, then drift again. Watching her was like watching a supermarket trolley with a wonky wheel, technically moving forward but colliding with every display in sight. As maddening as it sometimes was, that wobbling was her way of discovering where the edges were. My job was to be the one standing nearby, ready to help her up and send her back out again.

I didn't always get that right. In fact, I mostly got it wrong. I became the storm she was trying to escape, and it's taken me years to admit it. Her feelings came in waves I didn't know how to ride. Instead of calming the water, I jumped in and started thrashing. Sometimes out of fear, sometimes out of sheer frustration, and often because I had absolutely no clue what else to do. If she raised her voice, I raised mine higher. If she shut down, I slammed the door on my own side. We clashed daily, both convinced we were right, and neither willing to budge. Then one day she looked me in the eye and said, "I wish you could be like other mothers." That cut deep.

I'd love to say Michaela was critiquing my oversized sweatshirt and leggings that didn't quite match her idea of a "cool mom." Or that she was thinking of those mother–daughter duos who shop, brunch, and post selfies captioned #besties. But it wasn't that. Not even close. What she really meant was, *I want more calm. I want space to say the messy thing without you trying to fix it. I want you to believe I'm good even when I'm not at my best, because that's what I think other mothers do.*

I didn't hear that, of course. I made it about me instead. Poor me, the inadequate mother. Poor me, never enough. Poor me, raising a daughter who clearly wished for another family. Once I'd cast myself as the victim, I wore the label *Not Like Other Mothers* like a scarlet letter and built my defence. If she wanted a courtroom, I could argue. If she wanted fire, I could deliver. It was absurd, and it hurt us both.

The logic that followed was equally absurd but oddly convincing. If she could handle parties, friendships, and shopping for her own shampoo, then surely she could handle her emotions without me. And when she couldn't? Off came the tragic-actress mask and on went the cross-examiner. "What do you even know about other mothers?" I'd snap. "Do these mythical creatures bring your forgotten instrument to school at seven a.m.; cook your favourite dinner after you've yelled at them; sit through a thirty-five-minute saga of who said what about whom; drop everything to drive you to a party you only remembered five minutes ago?"

Once I let anger drive, it didn't stop at the speed limit. It brewed, twisted, and hardened into something worse. I'd feel myself morph into someone I barely recognised: sharp-tongued, defensive, and determined to win. And then, out of that fog, came a thought no mother wants in her head: *Why can't you be like other daughters?* Even now, it makes me wince. We love our children as they are while also imagining who they could be, and in that gap, careless words can slip out, leaving scars we never meant to make.

What unfolded between us wasn't a rough patch; it became a loop. She'd collapse into tears or rage, and I'd rush in with fixes or match her fire with my own. Then came the guilt, and the cold distance that follows when nobody gets what they need. We were both reaching, but somehow always missing. Hurt. Repair. Hurt. Repair. Hurt. Hurt. Withdraw. Silence.

I'm not sharing this with pride. I'm sharing it because this is the side of parenting we rarely talk about, the side where love is steady, but tempers flare and leave everyone raw. It's easy to say we're teaching our kids to manage their emotions; it's harder to admit how often we stumble over our own. What I didn't see at the time was how lonely that must have felt for Michaela.

She reminded me of that when she was proofreading this chapter. She looked up and said, "Mom, it's good, but you haven't really touched on my feelings."

"I thought I had," I said. "What do you mean?"

"You're just skimming the surface," she replied. "Now that we've moved past it, could I tell you what it felt like for me?"

I was surprised by her words, but she was right. I had been so caught up in the heat of our clashes that I missed the rawness of her experience. As I wrote back in Part I, reactions are only the tip of something deeper. Beneath what was loud and visible was her quiet desperation to make sense of her world and herself, and I probably didn't know the half of it.

I wish I could forget what came next, but I can't. Her truth is part of our story, and I share it because maybe it'll stop someone else from making some of the mistakes I did.

With kindness and startling maturity, Michaela trusted me with some of her most vulnerable thoughts and feelings from that time. She told me about the fear that she would never feel "normal," the shame about moments she wasn't proud of, and the frustration of wanting to break the pattern but not knowing how.

She talked about the ache of feeling misunderstood and the loneliness of thinking no one was really trying. Worst of all was the heartbreak of believing she was the problem in our home, a belief I had too often helped cement with throwaway lines like, "She's such a drama queen" or "That's Michaela being Michaela." She described sitting on her bathroom floor, convinced she was failing at being a person, certain that she was "too much." Most days, she wasn't fighting me so much as the noise inside her head and the relentless story that she had to be perfect at feeling, performing, and pleasing.

Her honesty undid me, and I found myself with so many questions nobody can answer. Why is this so hard? If we love them this much, why is it so difficult to draw alongside and give exactly what they need? Why couldn't I set aside my fear and meet her where she was?

If I could rewrite that moment, I would have gone straight to that bathroom floor. I would have taken her hand and told her she was never the problem. I would have wrapped her in calm when mine was missing, spoken words when hers wouldn't come, and made sure she knew, beyond all doubt, that she was loved and never alone.

Looking back doesn't rewrite what happened, and it doesn't take away the ache. Still, I am grateful for Michaela's honesty, for her grown-up insight, and for the fact that we are both healed enough now to really hear each other. What I've gained from all of it isn't some neat sense of redemption or closure, but something that lives in the way I show up now, with softer edges, better questions, and a steadier centre that can hold both our feelings without needing to fix them.

When I think about it now, the difference between her hurts and mine is that her missteps were practice, while mine carried the weight of adulthood and left marks I never meant to make. From where she stood, I can see how she might have longed, even for a moment, for someone else's mother. I don't blame her.

The grown-up job is to keep seeing the good in our children, so trust has a chance to grow. Naming the imbalance didn't remove the ache, but it showed me what to do with it.

That doesn't mean we should stand passively and absorb every outburst. It does mean that emotional regulation is far messier than any neat checklist would suggest. It's not them versus us. It's a cycle of learning and unlearning, breaking things apart, piecing them together, talking, repairing, and trying again. In that cycle, we're the ones who set the tone. That's why the groundwork in Part 1 matters so much. If we can't sit with our own emotions, notice what's happening inside us, and steady ourselves, moments like these will swallow us whole.

If you're parenting a teenager, you may recognise yourself in some of this. You might be somewhere between *Will we survive this?* and *Where is the refund counter?* Take heart. It gets better, not because teens stop being intense, but because we learn how to stand with them without disappearing ourselves.

The reason I've told Michaela's story in all its messiness isn't because it's the only version of adolescence; it's because it shows what happens when emotional growth isn't on the radar. When presence gives way to reactivity, both parent and child are left to flounder without a framework. I could have written about my third child and given you a far prettier picture, one where I'd learned enough about emotional intelligence to do things differently. But that wouldn't tell you what's at stake if we don't learn.

I've chosen the harder story because that's where the lesson lives. Presence over perfection isn't a slogan; it's the difference between being swallowed whole by the storm and learning to steady yourself long enough to guide your child through it.

On the other side of that season, our closeness feels hard-won in the best way. We can smile at those battles now: "Did we really say that? Survive that?" because they taught us how to stitch a torn moment back together. We learned when to step in, when to stand back, and how to say, "I'm sorry." Repairs became our ritual, and over time those small, faithful returns turned into something sturdy enough to hold us both.

Those years showed us that unattended feelings gather weight. The discipline is to listen without rushing to fix, and to speak without aiming to win—habits that keep paying dividends in every other relationship we touch.

That's the hidden gift of the hardest seasons: they don't just shape your child; they reshape you. It's not glamorous, and it's rarely tidy, but it's the kind of growth you wouldn't trade for anything.

NOT MY FINEST SEASON

There are some chapters you don't exactly want to revisit, but you know you probably should. The ones that sit quietly at the back of your memory until something small, like a familiar road or an unexpected song, taps you on the shoulder and says, *Remember me?*

This sits somewhere between regret and growth, that uncomfortable middle bit where you can finally look back and think, *Oh, that's why I reacted like that?*

That memory was the result of a wrong turning where I ended up on "that road," the one I'd pulled onto years earlier when I literally ran away from home. A grown woman, fleeing her own family. It was something I said I'd never do, yet there I was, a mother who had quietly reached breaking point.

I think every soon-to-be parent should be issued a warning that the words, "I'll never...," will come back to haunt them. I sometimes hear my grown-up children say things like, "When I'm a parent, I won't ..." "My kids will never..." I just nod politely, the way you do when someone hasn't yet met the toddler version of themselves. I don't lecture. I'll let life handle that part for me. The point is that

I ran when I would have judged anyone else who'd even contemplated doing the same.

It happened during one of those turbulent moments I just described. Michaela was in full teenage meltdown; I was knee-deep in my own; Neil was attempting to be like Switzerland; and the boys were standing helplessly in the middle of it all. Desperate to escape the escalating emotion, I grabbed my keys, muttered something I can't remember, and bolted, with Michaela right behind me, clutching the door handle and begging me not to go. But I couldn't stay. I'd hit the kind of wall that doesn't bend.

It wasn't just exhaustion. It was an avalanche of sadness, frustration, desperation, regret, and fear, and it hit me all at once. And that's how I ended up in a random cul-de-sac, sobbing until I felt hollow, as though every bottled-up fragment of emotion had finally spilt out.

Even now, writing it leaves a tug in my chest. I hadn't just lost my temper that day; I'd lost myself. I knew it, Neil knew it, and our three children felt it too. Coincidentally, or maybe not, it was around then that the neighbours put their house on the market and moved. And honestly, I couldn't blame them. If you were raising a three- and five-year-old and your evenings were soundtracked by a teenager yelling, a mother yelling back, and a general sense of emotional carnage, you might start browsing for a quieter postcode too.

Could I not remember my own teen struggles—the constant feeling of being misunderstood, of wanting space and comfort in the same breath, and of pushing people away just to see if they'd fight to stay? I'd lived that. I knew that ache and at times can still feel it somewhere deep, like muscle memory. But somewhere along the way, adulthood crept in with its lists and logic and responsibility, and I forgot what it was like to feel everything all at once and not have the words to explain any of it.

What I couldn't see then was that behaviour is only ever the surface story. This bit spills out when everything underneath has nowhere else to go. Michaela wasn't being difficult for the sake of it; she was overwhelmed and completely flooded with feelings that were too confusing for her mind to sort through. I kept trying to fix it or reason with her so that we could go back to normal, whatever that is. Really, she needed me to be the grown-up, and I see that now.

Today, Michaela is a woman of remarkable strength and insight, wise beyond her years yet still curious enough to keep learning. I am proud of who she has become, but also of how she allowed me to grow alongside her. As much as I refused to give up on her, she never gave up on me either. That's no small thing. She had every reason to turn away, but she didn't. She chose to keep trying. Our relationship didn't mend overnight; it was rebuilt slowly through long, sometimes awkward conversations where we admitted the parts we got wrong and dared to name what we were really feeling.

We still clash sometimes. Old defences rise up, and we both have to remind each other that we aren't who we were then. We don't need to build walls just because we remember how much it hurt before. We're both still learning and growing, but what we gained from that season is something solid to stand on in the seasons to come.

There were so many layers I missed, but the ones that stand out the most were...

Playing the fixer.

I thought my role was to solve the problem, or maybe, if I'm really honest, to solve *her*. It never quite occurred to me before, but as I write, it feels true. I was so practical and so eager to fix what I perceived as broken that I jumped in with advice, laid out plans, and told her what I thought she should do, be, or feel. There was probably a place for that, just not then. What she needed wasn't a fixer or a foreman with blueprints; she needed a mother who could sit beside her and feel what she was feeling without trying to tidy it up.

I don't think I trusted myself to do that. I was afraid that if I opened the door to all that emotion, I'd drown in it too. But when I picture myself in her shoes, I know that's the kind of mother I would have wanted—someone who could hold the mess without making it smaller. I wish I'd known how to give her more of that.

Allowing pride to take a toll.

There was a time when being right, or at least being seen as right, mattered more to me than anything else. It stood quietly in the corner, arms folded, blocking the way to repair. Too often, I'd hold the ground, waiting for her to apologise first, even when I knew, deep down, that I'd gone too far. My responses weren't helping her understand what she was feeling or how to make sense of it all; they were really just me trying to prove a point and teach a lesson I thought she needed to learn.

Parenting isn't about sides. It's meant to be teamwork, with both of us working on the problem together. Pride has no place in that. It erodes trust, drowns out encouragement, and leaves little room for empathy or humility. When pride leads, we end up acting like opponents, when what we really need is to be on the same side.

Being inconsistent.

I may sound like a terrible mother (and there were plenty of days I believed that), but that's not the full picture. At the heart of it, there was real love and genuine attempts at understanding. I kept trying, and when I got it wrong, I tried again. I loved her so deeply, and watching her struggle felt unbearable.

The trouble was my consistency, or rather, the lack of it. Some days, she got the calm version of me, the one who could listen and hold it together. Other days, she got the sharp-edged one who snapped and took everything personally. I could be her safe place in one breath and undo it all with the next. I never meant to, but that kind of unpredictability doesn't build trust. It leaves the other person on edge, not knowing who will show up next. Is it the kind, steady mom who listens, or the I've-had-enough mom who is already out of patience? How is a child supposed to tell the difference? How much can they risk saying or feeling when they have no idea which version of you they will meet?

It's no wonder she froze me out at times. I used to take it as punishment, but looking back, what else could she do?

Feeling sorry for myself (woe is me).

Unprocessed emotions have a way of turning a mother into the tragic heroine of her own story. I know, because I played that role often. My inner script went something like: *Poor me. Look at all I do, and this is what I get in return.* It's not a flattering admission, but it's the truth.

Was Michaela really doing anything *to* me? Was she targeting me, trying to make my life a misery? Of course not. She was throwing her emotions on the table, saying without words, *Help, I don't know what to do with this.* And there I was, picking through the mess of her feelings, holding up the worst bits as proof that I had failed somehow, or that I was just too tired, or that life had handed me an impossible hand. That way of seeing things shrank my empathy and magnified my hurt.

Michaela wasn't the adult; I was. And just as you don't leave the maternity ward with a "no returns" slip tucked into the nappy bag, teenagers don't arrive with weekly memos explaining what's normal or how to cope. Nor should they. Their world is already heavy enough with self-focus and survival. They don't need to carry ours, too.

Mimicking bad behaviour.

This is immature parenting at its absolute best. I can't quite believe I'm even admitting it, but here we are. In some of my less-than-stellar moments, I would actually mimic Michaela's behaviour. Like, genuinely copy her tone or pull the same face back at her, sometimes with an added slice of sarcasm just to drive the point home. What even was that?

If Michaela came home sullen and withdrawn, I'd somehow decide the best approach was to meet her right there in the gloom, almost as if to say, see how you like it when someone else stomps around sighing dramatically. I mean, honestly. What did I think was going to happen?

"What's wrong with you, Mom?" she'd ask, exasperated. "Why are you acting like that?"

I'd shrug like nothing was off, when really, I'd added another layer of emotional confusion to the already volatile mix. Instead of connection, I pushed her even further away.

If you're walking this road with a teenager, it can feel impossibly hard at times, but it's harder for them. We know what those hormonal surges feel like, the ones that hijack sleep, mess with moods, and flood the body with feelings it can't name. We remember the confusion of friendships, identity, expectations, and how much it all hurts. If I could offer any advice, it would be to avoid making things more complicated than they already are. If that sounds like I'm preaching, please know I'm mainly talking to myself. I'm not assuming anyone else has stooped to my level here. You might have thought about it, but you probably didn't actually commit to the role the way I did. It's not a role you want. Trust me on that.

Today, Michaela and I have the kind of relationship she once wished for, the one she thought "other mothers" did better. The irony is, I'm still not like other mothers, and she's realised that's probably for the best. What we've built is ours, and that makes it infinitely stronger.

So no, this wasn't my finest season, but it taught me so much about the value of being present. It also taught me something important, something I want you to hear too. No matter how harsh the battle, it is worth persevering. It is worth admitting when you got it wrong and showing how willing you are to try again. Nothing says *I value you* more than that. Maybe that was what made the difference in the end. Getting it right every time was never the goal. What mattered was being willing to keep showing up. That is what shaped us into the mother and daughter who can now, without irony, write #besties.

IF I COULD DO IT OVER

Most of us parent from the surface, reacting to what's said, what's shouted back, and who slams the door first (or in my case, who gets in her car and screeches off like Lewis Hamilton). That's all information, but it's not the full story. Beneath the noise are layers of emotional energy that shape how we interpret the world around us. When we stay at the surface, we react to behaviour; but when we understand the state beneath, we respond to being. That small inner shift changes everything.

I know this sounds like advanced parenting theory, but it really does change how you see both your child's and your own emotions. One day, you'll catch yourself mid-argument thinking, *Wait, this is just a level clash,* and you'll silently thank me.

If you think about these emotional layers, the heavier ones like guilt, shame, and despair sit closer to the ground. Then comes anger, still uncomfortable but full of movement, and often the first flicker of life after the numbness of despair. Beyond that are courage, acceptance, love, and peace. None of these make us better people; they simply give us a little more room to breathe. When you picture these layers as something we can move through, it becomes easier to believe we are never truly stuck where we are, and neither are our children.

When your child is sitting in fear or anger and you meet them with guilt or frustration, you're both stuck in the same emotional basement, wondering why the lights won't turn on. You can't calm a terrified child if your own energy hums with anxiety. You can't guide them out of shame while drowning in your own. Someone has to reach for a slightly higher step, not to pull the other up, but to hold steady long enough for them to find it themselves.

That's what I eventually learned, though it took years and more than a few emotional cul-de-sacs. Michaela was caught in fear and anger, trying to make sense of a world that didn't feel safe. I was tangled in guilt and shame, convinced I was failing her. We were both climbing the same ladder, just on different rungs. The work was never about changing her mood; it was about shifting the energy between us.

Once you start to see this, behaviour begins to look less like defiance and more like communication. You start to rec-ognise your own reactions as energy too. You pause because you can feel what state you're in and sense what they need from you. Emotional energy is contagious, and the calmest person in the room really does steady everyone else.

I've mentioned Pollyanna before, but she's worth revis-iting here because she explains this part of the story perfectly. Whenever I was miserable, my mother would ask, "What would Pollyanna find to be glad about here?" It drove me mad, and I never understood why. Now I do. She was speaking from a calmer place while I was stuck in anger. We weren't wrong for being in different states, but we were speaking different languages. She offered light when I needed understanding. I didn't need her to cheer me up; I needed her to sit beside me in the dark until I could see the light myself.

That's what I wish I'd remembered with Michaela. When she was trapped in fear or rage, she didn't need my logic or positivity. She needed me to stand near her chaos without being pulled into it, to bring the energy of safety instead of control, and to hold the edges of her feelings until she could breathe again.

Understanding where we and our children sit in these emotional layers changes everything. It teaches us to meet emotion without matching it and to model steadiness that helps them rise. Our job isn't to drag them up the ladder but to stay close and steady until they can find their next step.

Learning this has changed more than how I meet my children and their emotions. It's given me a deeper awareness of my own and of those around me. Even in ordinary moments, like chatting over dinner, I notice the difference. With a few gentler questions and a bit more curiosity, I can see where the other person really is and where I am too, which makes for far better connection.

There's so much I now know that would have helped me. Hindsight, right? If I could go back and do things differently, I would...

Create space before reacting.

Oh, the difference a pause can make. Sometimes it's as simple as saying, "Could you give me a moment to reset before I respond?" Other times, it's an excuse to fetch a glass of water because you know that if you don't, whatever comes out next will only make things worse. That space matters. It gives your nervous system a chance to catch up. When you put words around it, it doesn't feel like abandonment. You can say, "I want to hear you. I just need a minute to calm down, so I don't say something I'll regret. I'll be back soon." The "coming back soon" is an important part of the communication process, so they are not left wondering if you've bailed or are having an emotional crisis. That mix of space and reassurance gives everyone room to breathe. Without it, boundaries blur, and everyone gets swept up in the storm.

Lead with kindness.

We talk a lot about boundaries and consequences, and yes, they matter because they keep the chaos from swallowing us whole. However, kindness makes them land safely. It's the difference between a wall and a bridge and shows up in a softer face, a slower breath, and a voice that says, *I'm on your side, even now.*

There were days I managed that, and others when kindness packed its bags and left the building. When she was crying and I was vibrating with frustration, gentleness felt impossible. I imagine that it's that level of kindness she believed was missing and part of the "why can't you be like other mothers?" response. It's what she needed and what I wasn't giving enough of.

Kindness could have looked like, "I can see you're dealing with something big right now, but I'm not in the space to respond. Could I take a moment, so I don't say something unhelpful?" It's honestly just communicating feelings so we can help them with theirs in the best way we can.

It could have sounded like, "What you just said hurt me. I know you didn't mean it, so I'm going to give us both some space to cool off." Best of all, kindness could have sounded like, "I love you, and because I love you, I need a breather before I come back to this conversation."

When you look at it through the lens of those energetic layers we talked about, what we are doing is creating that movement of emotion, from resistance to understanding and from frustration to care. It's kindness in motion. I love that.

Put connection before correction.

When Michaela felt seen, she softened. When she felt judged, she braced. It really was that simple. I used to think the answer was correction, that if I found the right words or the perfect consequence, she would finally understand. What I didn't realise was that logic never reaches a child who feels unseen.

Over time, I learned that connection opens the door to understanding. When I slowed down and said, "I can see you're overwhelmed and angry. I get it. I'm here," the fight started to lose power. It wasn't instant harmony, but it shifted something between us.

Connection isn't about agreeing or letting things slide. It's about staying human when everything in you wants to retreat into control. When a child feels seen, they can stop defending and start listening.

Help dim, not switch off.

If I could go back, I wouldn't approach Michaela's emotions like switches that were either on or off. At the time, there was a certain logic to pushing for the "off" switch, as if fewer emotions would mean fewer headaches. Except emotions don't vanish just because we want them to.

Trying to silence feelings is like putting a lid on a boiling pot and pretending it's under control, even as it rattles on the stove. The work is to guide their movement so they can flow without flooding everyone in the process. That's where the idea of the dimmer comes in. Instead of extinguishing emotion, we need to help soften it.

When a teen is already at a ten, dragging ours up to ten too doesn't help anyone, least of all a brain that is still trying to wire itself together. But if we can hold steady enough to bring things down to an eight or even a seven, it's still loud and messy, but it's no longer chaos.

These days, I try to stay present long enough for the dimming to happen, for them and for me. Sometimes I am the one at a ten, muttering to myself about how I'm supposed to be the adult here. But when I can catch myself, something shifts, and I find myself with more space to try again.

Model emotional presence.

If I could go back, I'd start with me. I wouldn't expect Michaela to manage her emotions if I weren't managing mine. You can't lead someone to a place you're not willing to go yourself. If I'd been able to name my own feelings more honestly, it might have stopped being about control and become about awareness. That kind of modelling could have been the real lesson.

I wish I'd paid more attention to where I was sitting on that emotional scale I talked about earlier. Was I stuck

in guilt, fear, or frustration, or was I moving towards courage and acceptance? It sounds like therapy homework, but
I think it would have grounded me. Once I recognised my
own state, I might have been able to shift it.

Children read us before they listen to us. If I'd been able
to bring calm into the room instead of tension, she would
have felt that too. That's the invisible exchange of energy
we don't always notice but always feel.

Emotional presence isn't about staying perfectly calm;
it's about being real enough to know where you are and
steady enough to find your way back. If I'd done that more
often, Michaela might have seen that it was safe to do the
same.

Apologise and repair.

I wish I'd stopped pretending that I always knew what I
was doing and owned it when I got it wrong. I wasn't trying
to be difficult; I just didn't know how to apologise. A simple, "I'm sorry I snapped. You didn't deserve that," would
have gone a long way. Maybe it would have helped Michaela
see that I was still figuring things out too, that I had my
own unprocessed mess and was at least trying to face it.

I wish I'd offered smaller apologies instead of saving
them for the emotional equivalent of a season finale. These
days, I'm practising stopping mid-row and saying, "This
isn't who I want to be right now. Can we start over?" It's

awkward and uncomfortable, but it teaches humility and shows what repair looks like. I think the world could use a lot more of that, don't you?

Repair is rarely glamorous, but if we're willing to show up for the clean-up, they usually will too. And credit to Michaela here. When I finally started picking up the broom, she was there with the dustpan. I don't take that for granted.

Spend time in their world.

If there's one more thing I wish I'd done differently, it would be spending more time in Michaela's world instead of hovering in the background. This happens when we show interest in what they're interested in.

For a while, her world was makeup. She could have run her own salon. She'd try to draw me in, but I'd wave her off with, "That's not me," which, to be fair, was true. My entire kit was foundation, mascara, and eyeliner. But it was never really about makeup. It was an invitation to connect, and I missed it. Maybe if I'd spent more time in that space with her, she might have shared more of what she was feeling before it grew too heavy to hold and came out sideways. A teen's interests are among the greatest doorways to real connection (and actually, this holds true for anyone).

If I could gather all these lessons into one truth, it would be this: what our children need most is presence. They don't need us to get it right every time or to share all their pas-sions. What steadies them is knowing we will keep return-ing. We pause when we need to, soften when we can, repair when we miss it, and sometimes, simply pull up a chair in their world, so they feel less alone.

From here, I want to share some of the simple tools and practices that helped me stay steady, so that when your own hard moments come, as they surely will, you'll have more to lean on than I did.

TOOLS FOR EMOTIONAL GROWTH

When I talk about tools, I don't mean a survival kit with a step-by-step manual or a laminated chart to decode every version of "fine." If only it were that simple. What I've gathered here is a handful of things that helped me steady myself and stay connected to my teens. Some worked straight away, others landed years later, and a few I had to adapt on the fly.

Think of this chapter less like an instruction book and more like rummaging through a box of possibilities. Take what fits, leave what doesn't, and don't be afraid to shape them into something that works for you and your family.

What ties them all together is the same heartbeat: to strengthen emotional connection, to see and understand each other more clearly, and to build relationships that feel safe and steady, even in the stormier years.

Tool 1: What Do You Need from Me Right Now?

It's a simple question, but one that can change everything.

When emotions run high, those words cut through the noise. They say, *I see you. I'm here.* No lectures, no interrogation, and no five-point plan, just presence.

It shifts the spotlight to them and reminds us that we're trying to meet *their* experience, not our tidy version of it.

There were times when Michaela was distraught, her emotions spilling out in ways that didn't make sense, but when I asked, "What do you need from me right now?" the atmosphere shifted. Sometimes the answer was gentle: "I just need you to listen." So, I sat quietly while she poured out what she couldn't yet untangle, and somewhere in the spilling, she found her own clarity.

Other times, she surprised me: "Can you give me some advice on what to do?" That was my invitation, not to assume, but to contribute when asked.

On harder days, the reply was blunt: "I need you to leave me alone." Painful as it was, that, too, was clarity; honouring it showed her I respected her boundaries, even when it stretched mine.

This small question slows us down before we rush into their storm with our own noise. It keeps us curious. Sometimes they'll know what they want; sometimes they won't. Either way, the question opens a doorway to connection without pushing them through it.

In my mind, that's as close to perfection as parenting gets.

Tool 2: Corner Time

Before you picture a sulking child in a "naughty corner," take a breath. Corner Time isn't punishment; it's survival, and dare I say, sanity.

The idea was born on a trip abroad when Michaela and I shared a tiny hotel room. One double bed, two people, and a long, tense history. I was nervous. The set-up felt like a recipe for disaster, so I came up with what I called "Corner Time." Either of us could call it whenever we needed to, no explanations or justifications required. "Corner Time" meant *I needed a breather.* It didn't even require leaving the room, more like quietly announcing, *I've built an invisible force field; please respect it.*

Sometimes it lasted ten minutes, sometimes an hour. Occasionally, it meant headphones in, back turned, with a clear *do not disturb* vibe. The point wasn't what we did; it was that we didn't need to explain. When emotions run high, half the time we don't know what's going on inside ourselves, let alone how to explain it to someone else. This was the perfect solution.

Corner Time came home with us and quickly became a go-to way for the whole family to process thoughts and feelings. It's especially handy on holidays when too many personalities, hormones, and emotions pile into one house. Instead of snapping or storming off, we call Corner Time. Simple, respectful, and highly effective.

My favourite part is the reminder that emotions don't always need explaining. Sometimes they just need space. When we honour that space, the storm almost always passes more easily.

Tool 3: Out-Loud Check-In

I almost spared you a third mention of the Feelings Wheel, but some tools earn their repeats. This one adapts to any age or stage, which makes it too valuable to leave behind.

This time it's more subtle. Teenagers live in their Frank Sinatra era, determined to do it "my way." Tell, show, or suggest, and they're gone. My top tip? Go stealth. Use the tool yourself and let them notice.

By sixteen, Michaela didn't need another lecture on emotions. She needed me to *practise* what I preached. Teens can sniff out hypocrisy a mile away. If I wasn't pausing, reflecting, and naming my feelings, why would she?

One evening, after a stressful day, I sat at the kitchen table, pulled out our worn Wheel, and sighed. "I'm so frustrated. I feel like I'm about to explode." I scanned the Wheel until my eyes landed on "disappointed." With mock seriousness, I declared, "This has Muffingate written all over it." Her phone slid down. "Muffingate?" she asked curiously.

The Wheel had done its work. I retold the story in all its glory: Joshua's meltdown, my outburst, and the guest who never returned (what a surprise). I admitted how angry I'd been and how disappointed I was in myself for spiralling. I didn't sugarcoat it; I leaned into the drama because, if there's one thing teenagers love, it's drama. I picked words off the Wheel that matched my mood and delivered them with flair.

It wasn't a strategy session or a lesson. It was a shared moment where the roles flipped, and Michaela became my listener and ally. That one conversation opened the door to others. I realised that when I stopped pushing her toward emotional awareness and simply lived it myself, connection followed.

This approach lowers pressure, builds trust, and quietly gives them permission to do the same. If they join in, wonderful. If not, you've still regulated yourself and left the door open.

Tool 4: The Blob Tree

If you don't know the Blob Tree, you should. It's quirky, fun, and ideal for visual thinkers. Picture a giant tree filled with little blob-shaped characters in different emotional poses. They have no faces or labels, just simple shapes that somehow capture a whole spectrum of feeling.

The beauty is that it sidesteps language. You don't have to name or explain anything; you simply point and say, "That one, the blob slumped under the branch. That's me today." No lecture. No heavy analysis. Just a simple, non-threatening starting point.

In my work, I've seen it help teens who struggle to name their emotions feel deeply understood. For instance:

1. A blob sitting with its back to the group may suggest isolation or dejection.
2. A blob swinging carefree might show a longing for freedom, and the stuck feeling that comes with not having it.
3. A blob clutching the top branch with stiff limbs often captures "holding it together."

Once, I sat with an A-level student who was weighed down by study pressure and anxiety seeping into every corner of her life. I placed the Blob Tree between us and asked, "Which one feels most like you today?" Sometimes her finger landed straight away on the blob dangling off the edge or the one standing outside the group. Other times, she paused for a long while before tapping quietly. No explanation needed, just *this is me right now*.

That single tap becomes a gentle invitation:

1. Why that one?
2. If that blob could talk, what would it say?
3. If you could give that blob one piece of advice, what would it be?
4. Which blob do you wish you felt like?
5. What might help your blob move one branch over?

The blob becomes a doorway to connection without forcing emotional clarity. You're offering an imaginative place to land and then exploring it together. Often, that's all they need, a way to show you where they are so you can meet them there.

For the original *Blob Tree* resources (including licensed downloads and tools), please visit the official site: www.blobtree.com.

Tool 5: Table Talk

Table Talk was born out of sheer survival. Picture five people, all talking at once, trying to tell their stories over dinner. Nobody listening, everybody interrupting, and at least one person sulking because they couldn't get a word in. From that glorious mess came a game that folds feelings into the chatter.

Inviting teenagers to share emotions over spaghetti bolognese can be risky. It's also surprisingly fun. Over time, it's built a rhythm of honesty we didn't always manage in the rush of everyday life.

We keep it simple: a stack of emotion cards and one die. On your turn, draw a card and roll:

1. Roll a one: act out the emotion on the card. (Yes, even "despair." Prepare for theatre.)
2. Roll a two: share a time you've felt the emotion on the card.

3. Roll a three: skip the card and name an emotion you've felt today.

4. Roll a four: name one difficult emotion you've had today.

5. Roll a five: balance it with a positive feeling from today.

6. Roll a six: play director and nominate someone else to share.

The beauty of Table Talk is how it makes ordinary emotional language part of the evening noise. Some nights land deep, others dissolve into laughter; either way, it keeps us connected.

There isn't a single tool that works for every teen, every time. Some land beautifully, others flop, and occasionally a surprising mix sparks the best conversations. What matters is the message that feelings matter, and we care enough to show up and keep trying. Keep the conversation alive, however messy or unpredictable, and you're doing the real work of connection for this age and stage.

FREQUENTLY ASKED QUESTIONS

Q1. How do I get my teen to open up when they only give one-word answers?

Ah, yes, the classic "fine" or "nothing." It can feel like trying to interview a rock. The trick is to avoid pouncing the minute they walk in with "How was your day?"

Side-by-side moments work better. Try in the car, while you're cooking, or when they are next to you scrolling on their phone. Keep the pressure low. Offer your own small share instead of demanding theirs: "I felt stressed today, and walking home in the drizzle weirdly helped." That models openness without cornering.

Q2. What if my teen explodes with anger or slams the door instead of talking?

First, try not to take it personally (easier said than done, I know). I've had my own less-than-proud door moments, and they feel good for about five seconds before regret moves in. Anger often covers fear, overwhelm, or sheer exhaustion.

Give space for cooling because barging in mid-storm rarely ends well. Later, when the heat has dropped, circle back gently: "I can see you were angry. Want to try again?" That teaches that repair is always possible, even after fireworks.

Q3. How do I balance giving them space while still setting boundaries?

Think of it like an elastic band: too tight and it snaps, too loose and it's useless. Teens need freedom and structure, sometimes within the same five minutes. Space looks like respecting privacy and letting them process in their own way. Boundaries sound like, "You don't have to talk right now, but you can't speak to me like that," or "We'll pause this and revisit after dinner." Clear, calm, and brief usually lands best.

Q4. What if I feel like I'm losing connection with my teenager?

Connection in this season looks different. Seventeen-year-old Josh isn't exactly lining up to spend quality time with me, so I know that ache. What helps is starting in *their* world. I'll ask about something he's into, even if I don't have a clue what he's talking about. When I stay in his world for a while, I often see his body language shift; his shoulders drop, and he uncrosses his arms. That's my cue to slip in a gentle question or two.

I steer away from the standard "How are you feeling?" because that's basic code for shutdown. Being specific works better: "How are you feeling about hockey?" or "You seemed frustrated with your maths teacher. What happened?" The trick is in the wording. Open-ended questions leave space for real answers. Hand them the option of a one-word reply and trust me; they'll take it every time.

Q5. How do I talk about emotions without sounding like I'm giving a lecture?

Tone is everything. If it feels like a lesson, they'll shut down. If you use too many words, they'll shut down. If you compare them (you really don't want to do that), they'll shut down. If you choose the wrong time of day, they'll shut down.

Clearly, there are a few challenges to getting this right, but if you try curiosity instead of instruction, you may have a shot. "That sounded rough. What did it feel like for you?" or "I wonder if that felt more frustrating than scary?" Keep it light, keep it short, and don't force it.

Q6. What if my teen just doesn't seem interested in emotions at all?

Some teens act like feelings are optional extras. Don't panic. Just because they don't engage openly doesn't mean they're not watching or absorbing. Keep naming your own feelings in small, ordinary ways, keep the door open, and leave tools like the Feelings Wheel or Blob Tree where they can be found without fanfare. Sometimes it's not about forcing a conversation; it's about creating an atmosphere where emotions aren't strange or shameful. One day, often when you least expect it, they'll surprise you.

ESPECIALLY FOR YOU

If you haven't yet ventured into the teen years, you might be thinking, *Oh my gosh, what kind of mother loses her cool like that?* Surely, teenagers don't push your buttons to that extent.

They do. Sometimes. And other times, they're delightful and funny, and you find yourself wondering what all the fuss was about, right up until the moment they roll their eyes so hard you can hear it from the next room.

Parenting a teenager can feel like rowing across the English Channel in a wobbly dinghy while your neighbour's child glides past on a gleaming cruise ship. It can be maddening. But it's not you, it's not your child, and you can be certain that it's not the cruise-ship kid.

We're all wired differently. Some of us grew up with hugs, and others with "you'll be fine," or silence. Some teenagers manage on eight hours of sleep, and others survive on fumes. Hormones arrive like a polite knock for some, and for others like a marching band barging through the door. Add to that the friendship drama, school pressure, the group chat that never sleeps, a sibling who insists on breathing too loudly, the maths test, the missing hoodie, the coach's throwaway comment … it piles up quickly. No wonder our kids react in different ways.

We don't control the tides of adolescence. At best, we steer the boat. This is the oxygen mask moment, where you put the mask on yourself first so you can support them better. When emotions run high and you're already running on empty, old patterns creep in. You'll meet eye-rolls with attitude, match shouting with shouting, and possibly try the classic: *If I talk louder, they'll understand me better.* They won't. Not once will your teen pause mid-rant to say, "Thanks, Mom, that door slam really clarified your point."

It doesn't work like that. It never will.

The good news is you don't have to get it right every time. What matters is noticing the moment. Stop, breathe, and remember that when your teenager is spinning in their storm, they need someone to steady them. You can't do that if you are drifting.

Start by asking yourself:

1. What's happening for me right now?
2. Am I dragging my bad day, exhaustion, or stress into this moment?
3. What would help me reset so I can meet them with calm instead of chaos?

How you show up shapes not only your relationship with your teen but also how they'll handle emotions long after the storm passes.

While we're on the subject of showing up, let's talk about failure.

There will be moments when you'll be convinced you've messed it all up, when words fly out too sharply, or the silence stretches too long, and you're left staring at the ceiling thinking, *I've failed at this.* You haven't.

The danger is that once you call yourself a failure, you start living as if it's true. The sharp words and the resolve to "do better tomorrow" creep into the narrative to the point that it becomes self-fulfilling. You expect to get it wrong, so every stumble becomes "proof," and every hard moment feeds the case against you.

That story is sneaky. It pulls you away from your child before they've even had the chance to shut you out. It convinces you that connection is already lost when, really, all that's happened is a rough day between two people trying their best.

When the voice rises, pause and name it. *There it is again, the failure story.* Then remind yourself, *I showed up. I stayed in it, and for today, that's enough.*

Some days, showing up might look like taking a slow walk around the block before you head back inside. Other days, it might mean sitting quietly on the edge of their bed, saying nothing at all. Each small return is a declaration that you're still present.

Our children need parents who keep coming back. Who stay in the relationship after slammed doors and tearful standoffs. They need proof that mistakes don't make some-one unlovable.

Kindness is key, and failure will never be the truth about you. Take it as a reminder to pause and start again. What your child will value most is a parent who keeps returning to their side. That's what they'll remember, and that's what counts.

FINAL THOUGHTS

The teenage years with Michaela were my crash course in emotional growth. No book or workshop could have prepared me for the weight of those daily clashes, yet no classroom could have offered richer lessons either. Looking back, I sometimes wonder how our house survived. The walls still hold the story of slammed doors, raised voices, and the occasional dramatic proclamation that no one had ever had it worse, and that was true on both sides.

Michaela made me face myself in ways I never planned to. She showed me how quickly I could reach my limits but also stretched my capacity for patience and humour. Somewhere between the meltdowns and the reconciliations, I learned that survival sometimes looks like laughing at the absurdity, letting the storm pass, and remembering that even when she stomped away, she was still listening. I didn't need to chase her down and make the point again.

The biggest truth I've carried from those years is that connection with a teenager is fragile, not impossible. It starts to grow the moment we stop lecturing, start listening, drop the judgement, and admit when we've messed it up. "I got that wrong. Can we try again?" might be the most powerful parenting tool there is.

It feels right to end where we began, with value. Our teens don't just need to know we love them; they need to feel that we like them too. Do they know we find them interesting? Do they feel our delight in who they're becoming? Not in a cringeworthy way, but in the small, ordinary moments: a smile across the kitchen, a question that isn't half-distracted, an invitation to tell us about their world. When people feel liked, they tend to lean closer. It isn't always easy, especially when they give little back. But I'm learning to say it out loud, "I love you, and I really like being with you." Words like that, spoken often, sink deeper than we realise.

At the end of the day, that's what I wanted for her, and for me: a connection steady enough to be the place she'd return to when life felt heavy. That can only happen when you keep your own emotions in check, model how you steady yourself, and stop expecting them to manage the weight of your reactions. That's our job, not theirs, and thank goodness for that.

So no, it isn't perfection that carries us through these years. It's presence. It's the ordinary, steady choice to show up, to repair, to say the words out loud. That's what teenagers remember. And honestly, that's what counts. Michaela pushed me to my edges, but in doing so, gave me a profound gift: the gift of remembering that growth in families is shared. We don't just raise our children; they raise us, too. The legacy of those years is not the chaos we endured but the resilience we discovered in each other.

FOR SKIM LOVERS

If you've landed on this page first, I'm not judging. In fact, I'd bet good money you're either standing in a bookshop with a glazed look in your eyes, or at home hiding in the loo, hoping this will point you to some fundamental truths.

What you have in your hands is the emergency quick-hit version you can scan and gobble.

While these snippets are designed to help you breathe a little easier, the whole chapter is where the real gold sits. It's where you'll meet me, knee-deep in teenage storms, making mistakes, slamming doors, and slowly figuring out how to stay connected without losing myself. The good news is that I did all of that and still came out the other side, stretched but much closer to my teen.

So yes, skim away. This part is built for exactly that, but don't miss the deeper dive. It's proof that connection in the teen years isn't only possible; it's worth all the drama that comes with it.

When navigating your adolescent's emotions, remember...

It's a rollercoaster.

And nobody checked whether you liked roller coasters before strapping you in. One day they're independent, the next they want you close, and by evening you're back to being the villain.

Connection looks different.

Forget "How are you feeling?" That's an instant shutdown. Go where their interests are. Talk hockey, TikTok, or algebra, even if you don't get it. Connection often sneaks in sideways.

Conflict will happen.

Sometimes it's loud, sometimes it's sulky, sometimes it's both in the same hour. What matters isn't avoiding it but how you come back from it.

You're not a failure.

Those days when you lose it, when you say things you regret, when you wonder if you're cut out for this—they don't define you. What defines you is your willingness to reset, repair, and keep showing up.

Tools help.

Blob Tree, Corner Time, and Table Talk are each playful, practical ways to make sense of big emotions without forcing conversations teens don't want to have. None of it is magic, and some work better than others.

Boundaries are anchors.

Not punishments, not withdrawal, but invisible lines that protect both of you from spiralling further than you need to.

You grow too.

As they test independence, you learn patience. As they wrestle with identity, you discover resilience. As they practise emotional regulation (however clumsily), you practise it right alongside them.

THE TAKEAWAY:

Parenting teens isn't about controlling the storm or pretending it's not happening. It's about being the steady presence they can push against, retreat from, or come back to, knowing you'll still be there. The storms pass. What stays is the connection you've fought to keep, even when it was tested most.

Part V

Navigating a Young Adult's Emotions

THE HEART OF A YOUNG ADULT

In my head, young adulthood was going to be the grand finale, the moment I could proudly say, "Look at them, officially functioning adults who process emotions like seasoned therapists."

What I've discovered is that parenting and the emotional growth that goes with it isn't a stage we complete; it's a path we keep walking. I know that sounds terribly philosophical, like something I should have said with a shawl around my shoulders and a cup of herbal tea in hand. The irony is that I'm still untangling my own emotional spaghetti, tugging at knots that have been with me for decades. If I'm still at it, how could I ever expect them to be finished?

Yet, somewhere along the way, I stamped this stage "mission complete" and pictured myself quietly retiring from the emotional frontlines. In my imagination, there'd even be a handwritten thank-you full of insight, gratitude, and adult-level awareness to mark the occasion. Not a text or thumbs-up emoji, but an actual letter.

Not so fast. Teaching and growing don't end just because they're taller, live elsewhere, or have mastered the air fryer.

Life keeps unfolding with new jobs, changing relationships, unexpected turns, and hormones that never quite retire. In that swirl, emotions keep showing up, shaping choices, testing patience, and inviting us back into the same steady, imperfect presence that has always been at the heart of parenting.

Even with my longing for a finish line, there is still something deeply rewarding about watching your children grow into adults who can name their feelings and lean into hard conversations, even when they're messy or uncomfortable.

I'll be honest, I didn't always appreciate this growth, especially while still grappling with one who seems determined to make teenagerhood an advanced course in patience. What steadies me is remembering the work Michaela and I did when she was younger. We worked through big emotions and, in the process, built a connection we can lean on now. It's proof that when we put in the work, we do eventually get to see the growth. These days, I try to make more of a mental note of the wins. They keep me going in the quiet moments that no one claps for.

As any parent can tell you, every stage comes with its own knots to untangle, and young adulthood is no different. Reward and challenge aren't opposites after all. They travel together. The very moments that unsettle me are often the ones that grow us both, carving out deeper connection and shaping the resilience we will carry forward together. It's a chapter that, for all its messiness, I wouldn't trade.

Still, there's a part I keep stumbling over. After spending years running ahead with a metaphorical broom, sweeping away anything that might trip them up, stepping back feels almost unnatural. But that's exactly what this season asks of me: a quieter kind of influence, one where presence matters more than plans.

Technically grown, they're expected to make big life decisions while still figuring out who they are, what they want, and how to deal with everything life is throwing at them. Some days, it's genuinely impressive to watch them sort out their own admin, book appointments, and even string together complete sentences that sound almost parental. Other days, they're overwhelmed, avoidant, and reacting as if they've only just discovered what feelings are.

This is the tricky part, the *now what* space. How do we help them learn the art of navigating their own feelings? It sounds calm and straightforward when you say it out loud, yet in practice, it feels more like trying to hand over the steering wheel while the car is still moving. Given my instinct to keep a tight grip, it's no surprise that letting go without panicking is still something I'm learning.

That instinct didn't appear out of nowhere. For most of the past twenty-something years, my default setting has been to dive headfirst into my kids' emotional worlds. I've shown up armed with fixes, suggestions, soothing words, and the occasional "helpful" correction, convinced that it was my job. On the surface, it sounded wonderfully hands-on. In reality, it meant that as they grew older and started carving out their own paths, I was still trying to play a role that no longer quite fit.

I suppose you could call me an emotional meddler, a title I've only recently made peace with. At this stage, my meddling usually begins with a well-meaning but not-so-subtle, "You should know better by now," which, shockingly, has never been met with applause. When that lands flat, I move to act two: the dramatic, slightly passive-aggressive retreat, usually punctuated by a line like, "Fine, you're an adult, you decide." And because I like to commit to the full performance, there's always an internal encore, a moody soundtrack that sounds suspiciously like Celine Dion's *All by Myself*. It goes something like, "They don't need me anymore ... I've messed this up... maybe I was never that good at this in the first place."

I wish I were exaggerating.

Emotionally mature or not, it's not always obvious how we're supposed to show up for our young adults. This messy in-between stage is as maddening for us as it is for them, and there's no clear manual for it. What I am learning (usually the hard way) is that it calls for a slower, more intentional kind of presence. The kind that doesn't try to fix or fade into the background, but just holds steady and keeps the connection alive, even when the ground between us feels wobbly.

It helps, of course, to keep a sense of humour about the whole thing. Thankfully, Michaela has never been short on that. On the eve of her twenty-fifth birthday, she phoned me and said, "Mom, guess what's happening tomorrow?" This is a game we've played for years, and so I assumed she was referring to her birthday.

"I know, love," I replied. "You told me yesterday."

Her response was so perfectly Michaela that I couldn't help smiling. "Actually, tomorrow's the day my prefrontal lobe reaches full maturity." That's her humour to a T: dry, tongue-in-cheek, and genuinely thrilled at the idea of waking up with upgraded software.

To be fair, she wasn't wrong. The prefrontal lobe, the part of the brain responsible for planning, decision-making, and emotional regulation, typically reaches full development around age 25. She knew that brain maturing didn't mean instant enlightenment, but that didn't stop her from claiming it as a birthday bonus.

On the day of her birthday, we raised a glass to Michaela and her fully developed prefrontal lobe. There were speeches, jokes, and the celebration of emotional brilliance. We had fun with it, knowing full well that brain development is one piece of it, and the rest is practice, patience, and learning how to live inside the person you're still becoming.

That learning goes both ways. I've often thought parents deserve a prefrontal lobe upgrade of their own, something that adds wisdom, emotional restraint, and maybe even a feature that auto-deletes the phrase, *you're not needed anymore*. Still, this season holds so many quiet opportunities, and I'm only now beginning to appreciate that.

The pace is different here. Less frantic than the toddler years and less sharp-edged than adolescence. For me, the gift has been discovering the presence of a child who can sit with me, talk honestly, and share more of themselves than ever before. They show flashes of self-awareness now, moments of clarity about what's stirring beneath the surface. It doesn't erase my role as a parent; it reshapes it into something quieter, deeper, and every bit as precious.

With Michaela, this is where we've arrived. With Matthew, it's a space we're still learning to navigate together.

Matthew's story (and the chapter that's taken the longest to put into words) is still unfolding. I'm learning as I go, and Matthew and I experience emotions very differently. It's only now, with him firmly in young adulthood, that I'm beginning to see how he makes sense of his inner world, and that brings a quiet ache for the pieces I missed, the cues I misunderstood, and the emotions he kept tucked away.

There's a part of me that wants to push pause here and wait until I have more clarity, until I've figured out how this chapter ends, or at the very least what it's trying to teach me. But that wouldn't be honest. Instead, I'm writing from the middle of it, right where I am.

Perhaps that's what makes it worth sharing, because many of life's lessons don't arrive with tidy conflict or dramatic failures. Sometimes they come from loving someone so deeply that even a small oversight leaves its mark. That's what I've been carrying, the quiet ache of knowing I missed something that mattered.

This isn't the tidy version, and maybe it doesn't need to be. This is me, sitting in the middle of it, writing with my heart a little more exposed, and that's okay. Maybe what we need in seasons like this isn't a tidy conclusion, but the courage to stay present, to keep noticing, keep adjusting, and keep loving with the kind of open heart that never stops learning.

To really understand, I need to introduce you to Matthew, because understanding who he is and how he moves through the world is the only way to understand where I'm coming from and what it truly means to grow emotionally alongside your child, even when that child is no longer a child.

THE CALM I MISUNDERSTOOD

For a long time, I described Matthew as my easy child, and he genuinely was. By six weeks, he was sleeping through the night, taking daytime naps with little fuss, and happily entertaining himself for hours. There were no tantrums to speak of, hardly any drama. Naturally, I chalked it up to stellar parenting. What a mistake that was.

Six years later, Josh arrived, making it abundantly clear that while parenting plays its part, temperament gets a vote too, and often the louder one. That was the end of my smug phase and a lesson in humility well earned.

To avoid being ambushed by accusations of favouritism, I want to be clear that Matthew wasn't a saint in training. He was just an ordinary kid with his own quirks and moods. Still, compared to Michaela and Josh, Matthew's compliance felt like a gift. He moved through life at his own steady pace, while the rest of us charged at it, full tilt.

I don't know if Matthew was immune to the chaos around him, but from where I stood, his calmness looked like peace.

For example, Christmas at our home was a frenzy of stockings, presents, lights, and music. While everyone else tore through wrapping paper, Matthew would remove the Sellotape so carefully you'd swear it was part of the gift. Even as an adult, I had to resist the urge to nudge him along, mostly because I was itching for my gift too. The real test came when his present was a book. That's when everything came to a grinding halt. He'd simply start reading, oblivious to the growing pile of unopened presents and his restless siblings. Eventually, we learned to save the books for last.

That same patience showed up in his relationship with his sister. Whatever game she invented, he was there, loyal, easy, and happy to let her lead. One afternoon, in full teacher mode, with their cousins as students, she handed out test results. Matthew was the only one who received an F and was therefore sentenced to stand at the window while the others played outside. Remarkably, he did; he accepted the grade, the punishment, and the view as if it were all perfectly reasonable.

Matthew's calm could fool you. It looked like ease, like he was simply going along with whatever life handed him. But still waters have their own kind of movement, just quieter and almost invisible from the surface.

His willingness to go along didn't mean he wasn't thinking. If anything, Matthew was my deepest-thinking child, forever turning things over in his mind. There's one story that's become a family favourite, retold more times than I can count. We were all at the dinner table one night, deep in conversation about a high-profile murder trial, arguing over motives and verdicts as if the jury were waiting on us. Matthew sat there silently, listening—or so we thought.

Out of nowhere, he said, "I wonder why people build houses on floodplains?"

For a moment, we were speechless. Then the whole table erupted in laughter. That was Matthew, deep in thought, just not the same thought as the rest of us.

Sometimes I think of his mind as a private library. The shelves are lined with facts and theories, stories and feelings. Logic keeps the shelves from sagging. But emotions don't file as neatly. Sooner or later, they spill. And for him, that spill looked like self-doubt, hesitation, endless second-guessing, as if one wrong move might bring the whole library down.

By the time university came along, the shifts were harder to miss. He pushed himself to get everything just right, holding on so tightly you could almost feel the strain of it, as if loosening his grip, even slightly, might cause something to slip.

He also grew quieter, which I found unsettling. With Michaela and Josh, emotions were noisy. We argued, circled back, talked it through, and our mess was always out in the open. This wasn't the case with Matthew, and I took it as a sign that everything was fine. Except, fine, as I've already said, is a word that wears a hundred disguises.

The illusion cracked after he finished his engineering degree. The final stretch had been brutal, and I assumed once he was home, the pressure would lift. It didn't. Even with the deadlines behind him, small things triggered big reactions, and his responses felt intense and out of sync with the moment, as if those neatly stacked shelves had finally buckled.

The breaking point came after a game of golf. It was meant to be a casual game. However, in our family, "casual" usually means "wait for the competition to escalate." Sure enough, by the end, it looked less like a Saturday game and more like the world championships.

Matthew probably needed the win more than any of us realised, but it didn't happen. With emotions already stacked high, losing to his younger brother was the final nudge. The dam didn't leak; it burst. Years of quiet pressure and unspoken frustration came rushing out.

Returning home, he stormed up the stairs, nearly knocking me over as he made for his room. Moments later, there was a yell and a crash that told me that his bookcase had paid the price. This was not adult behaviour, not even close. I tried to ignore it, hoping he'd cool off and offer a sheepish apology. Instead, that not-so-adult behaviour escalated with banging, yelling, and heavier thuds—nothing destructive, but enough to make it clear that he was not fine.

At first, I reacted like any good mother who's just watched her grown son lose it after a game of golf. I got cross. Properly cross. I didn't like this loud, angry, and unfamiliar version of Matthew. It felt wrong, like someone had swapped out my calm boy for a stranger, and I wanted to shut it down. I was ready to barge in and deliver the "don't you dare behave like that in my house" talk. But the deeper thoughts were: *I don't like this version of you; it unsettles me, and I don't know how to deal with you in this state.*

And that's when it hit me. I'd spent years protecting him, smoothing things over, keeping calm and ensuring nothing was too heavy. I thought it was love, as if I was protecting him. But really, it was avoidance. I wasn't afraid he couldn't handle big feelings. I was afraid *I* couldn't. While there's a kind of sadness in that acknowledgement, the truth was enough to prevent me from rushing into his room with a lecture on how to behave.

Instead, I paused just enough to, you guessed it, check in with myself. It may have taken twenty-odd years, but I'd gotten there. *What do you need right now, Leonora?* And more importantly, *what does Matthew need right now?* I can tell you, hand over heart, that the pause lasted no more than a few seconds, but that was enough for me to make an intentional decision about what to do next.

As I entered his room, I was met with raw and messy emotions. Matthew sat crumpled on the floor, sobbing uncontrollably. His face was buried in his hands, clearly hiding from his own embarrassment. When he shifted to look at me, I caught a glimpse of his eyes, swollen from tears that he could no longer hold back. I'd never seen him like that. Sitting before me wasn't my six-foot adult son, but the six-year-old who had once spent hours curled on my lap, and in that moment, all I wanted to do was rescue him. That's when I realised that this wasn't a moment for plastering over or rushing to fix it. What he needed was space to feel the full weight of those painful emotions, which very clearly ran deeper than a round of golf.

It was only later that he admitted it hadn't been about losing the game at all. Golf had become the place he escaped to when life felt overwhelming—the fresh air, long stretches of green, and the quiet reward of watching the ball land exactly where he planned it. What he hadn't realised until then was how fragile that calm could be, and how quickly one game could take it away. Given how much he usually holds in, the way he explained it was encouraging. He didn't just understand the reason behind his reaction; he managed to put it into words with such clarity that it gave me a window into what he'd been carrying all along.

That moment changed me. It wasn't dramatic, but the way I saw him, and the way I saw myself as a parent, changed. I felt proud that he'd found his own words, but right beside that pride sat a quiet ache for everything I'd missed.

For years, I'd mistaken silence for calm, assuming that a steady exterior meant stability. I'd listened to what he said, not what he couldn't, and missed the stories that lived quietly inside.

It's almost easier to parent the child whose emotions are loud. You know where you stand with a toddler lying face down in aisle three or a teenager slamming a door so hard you fear for the hinges. Those feelings might be messy, but at least they're visible. You can meet them, argue with them, and even laugh about them later.

The ones who slip under the radar are different. Their silence is its own language, and I'm still learning how to translate it. It takes patience and a willingness to stay close even when there's nothing to fix. Their feelings are no different from anyone else's. They eventually surface, and when they do, they ask to be met with the same understanding we give the noise.

His silence was speaking a different language. If I'd been more aware, I might have noticed it. Matthew had been experiencing gut issues, fatigue, and bouts of illness that seemed to arrive without reason. Bessel van der Kolk, in *The Body Keeps the Score*, puts it plainly: the body carries what the mind suppresses. Looking back, I can see how true that was. His body was speaking long before his words did, and I missed the clues.

Psychologist Susan David's words also helped me make sense of this in that emotions are "data, not directives." They are not there to instruct us on what to do, but to show us what matters. I wish I had recognised that sooner, because when a child who has always kept their feelings hidden finally lets them out, it can feel overwhelming, even explosive, and that is precisely where Matthew and I found ourselves.

When I walked into his room that day, I knew that I couldn't fall back to my usual script of questions, advice, or that familiar tone of concerned authority. Perhaps most of all, I couldn't see him as broken, because he wasn't. He was caught in the middle of his own storm, yes, but he wasn't being destroyed by it. He was learning how to ride the waves, and as overwhelming as it was, this wasn't the end of something; it was the beginning of him making sense of it.

What I did next surprised even me, because it went so completely against my dive-in, fix-it, "do something" nature. Maybe this is the key to parenting a child who is no longer a child. Instead of rushing in with words or solutions, I pulled up a chair at his desk and simply sat down. That was it. I didn't speak. I didn't reach for the right thing to say. I didn't even ask if he was okay. I just sat in a room so heavy with emotion it was hard to breathe.

Time stretched on with neither of us saying a word. Do you know how hard it is to sit in silence while your child is overcome by his feelings? Every part of me wanted to leap in and make it stop. Doing nothing felt awkward, almost wrong, and yet, that was exactly what the moment asked of me.

I realised then that silence isn't the absence of sound; it's the quieting of everything inside us that wants to fix or flee. Even discomfort has something to say if we let it.

That day, I held it a little longer than I ever had before. I stopped filling the space with words. I stopped reaching for control. And in that quiet, something shifted. I was finally still enough to meet him where he was, and that made all the difference.

My not saying anything wasn't only new territory for me but for him too. Matthew is used to me having words, plenty of them. Advice, opinions, solutions—I have a ready supply. I could almost see the confusion on his face, like he was waiting for the familiar script to start. *Here she comes. The lecture. The life lesson. The mom voice.* But I didn't say a thing. I just sat there, quiet, calm, and uncharacteristically still. I can only imagine what he was thinking. *Where's the guidance, the reaction?* And maybe, when the silence kept stretching, *What is she expecting of me?*

In that space, something began to shift. Slowly, the deeper feelings rose to the surface. Shame came first. It always does with Matthew.

It strikes me that shame is the one emotion he can name easily. I think it's because, for him, it connects straight to his values, to the kind of person he believes he should be. When his behaviour slips outside that, even slightly, he feels it like a bruise. The guilt follows quickly, and then the self-blame. Those three speak the loudest, and when they do, they drown out everything else. They keep him circling the surface, unable to reach the gentler feelings that really need his attention.

I could see all of that playing out right there in front of me, the weight of it sitting heavy on his shoulders while he tried to swallow it all back. I stayed where I was, which felt impossible. Every instinct screamed. *Go to him, fix it, say something.* But his body was saying something different: *Don't.*

So I didn't.

After a while, his shoulders softened, his face lifted, and he looked across to me with what I can only describe as permission in his eyes. Even then, I had to respect the boundary and see the adult and not the child. His eyes seemed to say, *Love me. Be present. Just don't ruin the moment by diving in to fix.* I think that this was the first time in all my years of parenting that I saw the true value of this.

That day didn't end with tidy words or sudden insight. The full story of what unfolded next belongs with the tools I'll share later, because that's where the real understanding came. It's the best place to see how those tools work in practice, especially in a moment like this.

What I can say is that this was a turning point in how I parent. With Michaela, who has always been more independent and expressive with her emotions, there was less chance for me to interfere, so I never fully realised how often I was doing it. Only in practising that uncomfortable silence with

Matthew did I realise what I had been taking from him. From that point on, I began to see him differently. He was no longer the child I thought I had figured out, but a young man carrying emotions he was meant to process. I began to see myself differently, too.

THE QUIET WINS

The golf story could've gone completely differently. If I'd done what I usually do, we both would've missed the point. He would've missed his own feelings, and I would've missed the miracle of what happens when I just stay still.

That realisation was its own kind of win, the kind that sneaks up on you later when you're doing the dishes or driving alone, and you suddenly think, *Oh. That was it. That was the moment I changed.*

Looking back, I saw two things. The first was him, no longer the little boy with his head tucked under my chin, but a young man working hard to find his place in the world. The second was me, discovering that the world doesn't fall apart if I hold my tongue. I'd always imagined silence would mean distance, but I learned silence can be a bridge.

Nancy Kline says most listeners are trained to "insert, tailgate, or populate the silence" with their own views. *The Human Behind the Coach* describes real listening as letting go of "our own inner clambering." That racetrack of thoughts has always been my undoing. Stepping back showed me that I'm more capable of restraint than I thought, and there's strength in that kind of holding back.

What I offered Matthew was an intentional silence that gave him room to go deeper into himself, with the full knowledge that I was right there for when he was ready to speak. That, too, was a win, a quieter one, but perhaps more lasting. When you think about it, isn't that something we all crave? Not just the chance to speak, but the chance to feel that the other person has quieted their own noise long enough to truly listen. That kind of silence is rare, and it's worth noticing when it happens.

In the days that followed, Matthew carried himself differently. It was as though my staying still in his storm had made room for him to stand stronger. That slight shift opened the door to a win I hadn't anticipated.

He was reading a draft of this very chapter. He's in it, after all, and I wanted him to have a say. Halfway through, he paused, weighing his words. Then, with awkward bravery and startling kindness, he said, "Mom, do you know that you can be quite controlling?"

Oof. Not exactly the win I was expecting.

It caught me off guard. While it's not entirely new information, I would have preferred to be the one to say it, on my own terms, and preferably wrapped in a bit of humour to soften the edges. Hearing it from him brought its own kind of discomfort. "I know you mean well," he said with incredible sincerity. "I know it's because you care, and you don't want me to fail, but when you jump in too quickly, you stop me from learning. You've always told us that growth comes from mistakes, so why don't you let me make mine?"

One could call that a low blow, yet it was spot-on. My mind, ever quick on the defence, began lining up arguments, excuses, and explanations like a lawyer preparing closing arguments. So much for all the wisdom I'd gleaned from Nancy Kline and *The Human Behind the Coach*. In that moment, it seemed to have evaporated completely. Still, I caught myself quickly enough to notice the knee-jerk reaction for what it was. What Matthew was doing, in his own way, was handing my own wisdom back to me, and the discomfort I felt was nothing more than the realisation that I hadn't been applying it. In that honesty, he found the courage to tell me the truth, and I found the humility to hear it.

Maybe you've had a moment like that, when your child holds up a mirror you didn't expect, and you see something you've been avoiding. Rest assured, you're not the only one. Matthew wasn't pushing me away; he was asking me to step back and let him steer. "Stay in your lane, Mom, not because I don't love you, but because I need to know I can walk my own road without you clearing it first."

Being able to express that was just as much a growth moment for me as it was for him. The growing is never over for parents. My hair may be greyer and my history longer, but I'm still very much in the learning lane. What's at the heart of all of this is that we are not only raising emotionally aware children, but we are also choosing to be emotionally aware grown-ups alongside them. Getting it right, even for a moment, is worth celebrating.

After the golf course incident, home life returned to its usual rhythm, with one slight change. That day, I'd done something entirely against my nature. I found my voice, and then, in the name of progress, promptly shut it up. If you know me, you'll understand what a monumental feat that was. Normally, I'd have offered commentary, direction, and perhaps even a closing argument, but I stayed quiet, and that probably was the biggest win of all.

Matthew is still Matthew. He'll mull, ponder, and turn things over in his mind far longer than I ever would. The difference is that I've stepped back from trying to narrate his life like a voice-over. It's a work in progress for me, but one I'm learning to be at peace with.

Michaela, now the proud owner of her fully developed prefrontal lobe (which she continues to toast on birthdays), often phones when her emotions are changing lanes. She doesn't want me to take the wheel; she just wants me in the passenger seat while she decides which turn to take. That's a win too, a sign of trust and connection that grows stronger because I don't try to steer.

Then there's Josh, currently veering all over the emotional motorway with his indicators very much optional. I suspect his prefrontal lobe won't be *fully operational* until well into his thirties, possibly longer. His way keeps me on my toes, and when I remember to meet it with presence rather than panic, that's its own kind of win.

Three young adults, and three very different ways of moving through emotion. My role in all of it is to sit on my hands, breathe, and stay in the room without trying to tidy it. That's the job, and when I manage it, I find that the real wins are already there, waiting to be noticed.

WHAT'S STRETCHED ME

Our children don't turn into us; they turn into themselves. Now, isn't that a surprise? I'm being facetious, of course, but I sometimes think much of what we call parenting is really an unconscious attempt to mould them into smaller versions of ourselves, at least our better bits.

Still, there's something about control that feels … comforting. I like knowing what's coming. It's somehow tidy, perhaps a little predictable, and yes, safe. But kids don't live in boxes. The real stretch is prying open the lid and letting them out.

It's a bit like the whole learning-to-drive thing. With the first, I insisted on being the teacher. Huge mistake. We lasted about four journeys before we were both shouting over the handbrake in a supermarket car park. With the second, I gave up sooner and called in a professional. By the third, I didn't even pretend. Straight to the instructor. I may be a slow learner, but I do learn.

What surprised me is that the real stretch didn't come in the teaching. It came the day they passed their test, slid behind the wheel, and drove off without me in the passenger seat. Terrifying but not all that different from what we are doing now as we watch them begin to navigate their own world as adults. The stretch is real, but it's the only way to watch them grow into themselves.

Here's what that stretch has looked like for me...

Letting go without grabbing the wheel.

When bad news hits, or a job wobbles, or they end up in a relationship I'd have quietly sidestepped, it's their emotions that rise first. It may be fear, disappointment, anger, and sometimes all three. Mine aren't far behind. The urge to protect is still right there, like muscle memory.

It's hard to watch your child stumble, even when you know it's part of growing up. Every instinct wants to soften the landing. But that's not our role anymore. These days, my work is to stay in my lane, a phrase I've grown oddly fond of, mostly because it's true. The minute you drift into someone else's lane, you risk slowing them down or causing a crash.

Now I try to walk beside them instead, asking questions that help them find their own way. "What's going on? Tell me more? How did that feel? What did you do about it?" Simple questions, but they open doors that advice often shuts.

The stretch, for me, is standing still while they steer, watching them take roads that look uneven from the start, knowing I could warn them, maybe even stop them, but choosing not to. The hardest part is swallowing the *If they'd just* ... that hovers on my tongue. That's not my line anymore. My job is to stay close, love them through it, and trust they'll learn what they need to on the way.

Kicking the fix-it habit.

Every so often, they still hand me the reins with that look that says, *You sort it out.* Years of smoothing things over and quietly rescuing them have made me the obvious candidate. If I fix it, they don't have to risk getting it wrong; if it goes sideways, well, I'm right there to take the blame.

Recently, seventeen-year-old Josh had to drive himself to the airport. I explained where to park and which levels were for long-stay, short-stay, or meet-and-greet. From the glazed look I got in return, I knew he hadn't taken much in. The old me would have texted instructions, maybe even drawn him a map. This time, I chose to let it go. Mid-Zoom call, I heard him phoning Matthew, voice rising, clearly lost. Matthew didn't even pretend to help. "I'm not there, Josh. You'll have to figure it out." Click. And guess what? He did.

The win wasn't that Josh managed. It was that I didn't. I didn't fix it or jump in. I didn't even flinch. Okay, I flinched a little. But I stayed out. That's the work now, learning to unclench while they figure it out.

It's weirdly freeing, this letting go. I'm not lugging everyone's crises around anymore. And they're realising they can carry more than they thought. The bumps aren't failures; they're the work. They're how resilience is built. And resilience, I keep reminding myself, will serve them far better than a mother running a full-time emotional roadside assistance service.

Their emotions aren't my scorecard.

So apparently, I'm a recovering fixer now. Progress, right? Sort of. Because I still trip, all the time. The minute one of my kids gets quiet, mad, moody, or just off, I turn the spotlight straight on myself. *What did I do wrong? What did I miss? How did I screw this up?* And yet, when they're happy? I don't take credit for that. Their joy is theirs. Their pain, apparently, is mine.

It's ridiculous when you think about it. Somewhere along the way, I started treating their emotional weather like a report card. Sunny day? A+. Storm cloud? Try harder, Mom.

Mel Robbins says it best: *Let Them*. Their moods are not a reflection of me. They're simply living their emotional lives, which sometimes means slamming doors, sulking, or snapping for reasons that have nothing to do with me.

The stretch is remembering that their storms don't belong to me. I don't have to fix them, stop them, or stand in the rain with an umbrella yelling advice. I can just stay here, solid and dry, trusting that they'll find their own shelter.

Trusting them with their own growth.

With Matthew, I spent years treating his pain like a project, something to analyse, fix, and complete. If he hurt, I jumped in, like, *Move over, I've got this.* It felt like love. It looked like love. But underneath, it was fear that he couldn't handle it, that if I didn't hold him together, he might fall apart.

It took me far too long to understand that I was really saying, *You can't do this without me.* What I thought to be comfort was, in truth, a quiet kind of control.

These days, I'm learning a different kind of love, one that steps back without walking away. It's the love that says, *I trust you to do this your way, even if it hurts to watch.*

It's harder than fixing, much harder, because it means sitting still while they fall and trusting that they'll rise. More than anything, it's letting them know, without words, *I believe you can do this,* and that I trust their growth more than I doubt their pain. And somehow, that trust changes everything.

Tossing out my imaginary calendar.

If I had it my way, my children would move through life on a neat schedule, ticking off milestones with the efficiency of a project plan. University finished. Job secured.

Relationship stable. Emotional maturity fully installed. Done.

Life, of course, has other ideas. Growth comes in waves, rarely tidy, and never on my preferred timeline. The real stretch has been loosening my grip on that imaginary calendar and letting them grow at their own pace. Their timeline is theirs to own, and mine is to notice, encourage, and celebrate along the way.

What I am coming to see is that these stretches shape us, too. We learn to loosen, to steady, and release with more grace than we thought possible. Parenting doesn't stop when they hit adulthood; it just shifts into a quieter role. And while we cannot hand our children emotional maturity like a certificate at graduation, we can give them tools. They may not guarantee smooth sailing, but they just might make the path a little less overwhelming. That's what I am going to share next: the tools that have made the biggest difference in our family.

TOOLS FOR NAVIGATING EMOTIONS IN YOUNG ADULTHOOD

When our children cross into young adulthood, the emotional terrain doesn't suddenly smooth out. If anything, the feelings run deeper, and they're learning to steer through them mostly on their own. I've learned the hard way that you can't teach emotional skills by force. There's always that small, impatient voice that wants to say, *Just listen to me and skip the hard parts.* But it doesn't work like that, and it's not supposed to. Growth must be lived, not borrowed.

So instead of muscling my way into their lessons, I've learned to lay a few tools on the table and step back. They're not checklists or assignments, just quiet invitations to help them process and regulate when they're ready.

Tool 1: Hold the Frame, Not the Paintbrush

In the early years, we tie the shoelaces, fix the Lego towers, and supply the "right" words when they stumble. By young adulthood, those instincts are harder to switch off.

They don't need us to paint their picture anymore. They just need us to hold the frame steady while they paint.

We've already touched on holding space. Holding space means being present without rushing to fix, improve, or outdo their story with one of your own. It's sitting beside them in the mess without flinching, even when every cell in you is screaming, *I know a shortcut!* It's not easy, but when we resist the urge to rescue, we send a message no pep talk can match: *I believe you can handle this, and I'm right here while you do.*

If holding space is about presence, holding the frame is about structure. It's creating a steady, non-judgemental container where they can process without you painting over their picture. Ask curious, open questions like, "What's the hardest part about this right now? What do you most want to feel on the other side of this?" The frame keeps the focus on their process, not your solution.

When you're in the middle of a real conversation, these quick prompts might be useful:

1. *Understand:* "What feels most important for you to share right now?"

2. *Lighten:* "What would help take even a little of the weight off?"

3. *Step:* "What's one small step you'd feel okay taking next?"

With Matthew, I let the silence hang longer than I felt comfortable. His first response was, "Go away, Mom." Closely followed by, "Don't look at me." Fair enough; who wants an audience when they're wrestling with big emotions? My reply was simple: "I'm just sitting with you because I can see this is hard." Then I stopped and gave him enough room to meet his feelings on his terms, while knowing I was right there if he needed me.

When emotions spike, the brain's alarm system takes over and higher reasoning goes offline. If we rush in too soon, we meet the alarm head-on and often make it ring louder. Holding the frame gives the nervous system time to settle so the thinking part of the brain can come back online.

This doesn't mean sitting on your hands in silence forever. It means resisting the urge to jump in before they're ready. Sometimes the most loving thing you can do is to witness, reflect on what you're hearing, and let them wrestle with it in your presence. If they ask for your view, offer it gently and without attachment, leaving space for them to disagree or adapt.

For me, holding the frame means making peace with awkward silence, asking fewer questions than my curiosity would like, and trusting the quiet to do some heavy lifting. My role isn't to grab the paintbrush, but to keep the frame steady while my nearly grown children choose their own colours, even when they're not the ones I'd pick.

Tool 2: Put Feelings into Words ("Name It to Tame It")

Naming feelings hasn't outgrown its usefulness; it has simply grown up. What once was a way to calm a child is now a way for young adults to better understand themselves. The first word is often just the beginning.

After the golf game, when Matthew brushed past me and slammed his door, everyone saw anger, and if I'd asked him in that moment, he would have named it too. Anger is the easy option, the emotion that barrels to the surface and demands attention. Yet, like fire, it often hides what's smouldering underneath.

I knew that tackling the anger head-on would push him further away, so I stayed quiet, letting the silence do its work before gently saying, "Matt, I can see you're experiencing a lot right now. It's clear you're angry, but what else might you be feeling?"

Predictably, he circled straight back to anger. That's fine. I acknowledged it, then kept the invitation open: "I think there's more. Want to try naming it?" Slowly, the words began to come: embarrassment, because his behaviour didn't match his values; disappointment, because he felt he'd let us both down; and frustration, because he didn't know how to handle it all. Then came confusion, fear, and finally, relief. Naming things made space to breathe.

As he spoke, anger softened into something layered and human. At this stage, "Name It to Tame It" isn't just about calming down. It's self-regulation in action. Naming an emotion creates enough distance to choose what to do next rather than react on impulse. It moves them from being in the feeling to working with it.

From a coaching perspective, it also loosens the story they're stuck in. "I'm angry" feels like a full stop. "I'm embarrassed, disappointed, and frustrated" opens a new sentence. In our conversation, each word was like unlocking another room in a house he thought only had one.

The point isn't to push for a list every time. Sometimes they'll find one extra word, sometimes none. The power lies in offering a steady, non-judgemental space to look beneath the obvious emotion. In the young adult years, that invitation quietly says what they still need to hear: "I'm here. I'm not afraid of your feelings. And I believe you can handle them."

And sometimes, finding those words is easiest when no one's listening.

Tool 3: Journalling

Journalling isn't for everyone. Some take to it easily, others not so much. You might assume that, as a writer, I'd love it, and partly, I do. I like words, but I like sharing them even more. Writing into a void feels like shouting into an empty canyon. I process best when I can shape my thoughts and release them into the world. That act of sharing is my catharsis.

When I try to journal, I drift, circle back, or end up distracted. But I know many who swear by it, and Matthew is one of them. He doesn't keep a rose-pink diary tucked under his pillow, but I've seen the scribbles in his notebooks—quick, messy, and honest. For him, it's not about a perfect habit; it's about catching thoughts while they're fresh and giving them somewhere to land.

Writing things down can shift something inside. Tangled thoughts start to unravel, and patterns appear. Research confirms that translating experiences into language calms the brain's alarm system and lowers emotional intensity. You move from being *in* the feeling to *having* the feeling, and once you have it, you can decide what to do with it.

In coaching, we call this "defusion," creating just enough distance from thoughts so they stop running the show. A sentence on paper can turn an all-consuming storm into something you can stand beside instead of inside.

For young adults, the "right" way to journal is whatever doesn't feel like homework: daily notes, quick scribbles in challenging moments, a phone app, or even a voice memo. The goal isn't a beautiful record but a private outlet that doesn't need an audience. As parents, the most loving thing we can do is respect that privacy. No peeking, no summaries—just trust that it's their space to work things out.

Tool 4: The Inner Friend (Practising Self-Compassion)

When Matthew hit a low point after graduating, I watched him do something painfully familiar: turn on himself. "I'm so stupid," I heard him mutter. Then, "What's wrong with me?" He was furious *at himself* for feeling. I recognised it instantly. That instinct to attack yourself the moment you fall short. I've spent years unlearning it.

To help him understand, I shared that I've carried this struggle for years. There were times it felt like second nature to criticise myself, almost as if it were a sport I'd unknowingly trained for. I told him about the complicated relationship so many of us have with our bodies, the promises to "be good" next time, the nights when the fridge became a hiding place, and yes, even the comfort of an emergency chocolate stash. That part made him smile, which lightened the moment. Of course, I didn't reveal its exact location. Some things a mother is entitled to keep to herself.

Then I told him about the silent war in my head: *There you go again, Leonora, all-or-nothing eating; did you really think you'd be disciplined today? Failed again.* And the worst days, looking in the mirror and thinking, *I really don't like you.*

I asked, "What would you say to me if you heard me talk to myself like that?"

He didn't answer, so I did. "You'd tell me it's okay. You'd remind me that bad days happen. You'd probably make me laugh and tell me to stop being so dramatic."

His shoulders softened. That's when I said, "That's self-compassion."

It's not about excusing yourself; it's about softening the edges. People who practise it handle stress better and bounce back faster because they don't waste energy on shame. They see emotions not as proof they're failing, but as proof they're human.

My tall, slim son will never fight the same battles I have, but I shared mine anyway. Real connection happens when we drop the polished parent act and let them see the messy parts too. In the past, one slip would've sent me into a spiral of guilt and promises to do better. These days, I'm more likely to say, "Okay. That happened. Tomorrow's a new day."

The shift isn't just softer; it's stronger. When we quiet the voice that shames us and listen to the one that steadies, we save our energy for moving forward. Learning to rise without tearing yourself apart in the process is a superpower and one we should be passing on to our children every chance we get.

Sometimes I suggest something "coachy" but worth it: write a letter to yourself as if you were your best friend. I don't know if Matthew ever did this, but I've seen people change when they try: the tone softens, the words turn kinder, and something in them exhales.

Sometimes I model it out loud. I'll start with, "Ugh, I'm such an idiot." Then I'll pause and reframe, "No, wait. I'm a human who made a mistake. I'm fine." They get the point.

Encourage your young adult to notice how they speak to themselves, especially when life gets hard. If you hear them calling themselves "stupid" or "a failure" (or any of those sharp little daggers we throw inward), call it out gently. Ask, "Would you say that to me or your sister? No? Then why to yourself?" Share your own inner critic moments and how you're learning to answer with a kinder voice.

Life will throw them breakups, job rejections, and other curveballs. One of the best tools they can carry is an inner voice that says, *I've got your back, even when the world feels harsh.* Self-compassion says, *Feel what you feel. Don't beat yourself up for it. You're doing the best you can, and that's enough.* When they believe that, they learn they can fall apart and still put themselves back together, and maybe they'll believe it sooner because they've seen us practising the same thing.

Parenting young adults doesn't mean stepping out of the picture; it's about stepping differently. We still get to be there, just not with the answers. We hold the frame while they paint, help them name what's underneath the noise, give them a private space to untangle what's inside, and remind them, always, to be kind to the person they're becoming.

What lasts isn't how often we fixed it, but how we stayed, how we loved, and how we kept showing up.

FREQUENTLY ASKED QUESTIONS

Q1. What if my young adult doesn't want to talk at all?

That's normal. Sometimes the best thing you can do is simply be there, not lurking like a hawk, but available. Your quiet presence says, *I'm here when you're ready,* without the need for a grand speech.

Q2. How long should I "hold the silence" before speaking?

If it feels slightly awkward, you're probably in the sweet spot. Silence is uncomfortable for us because we think we should be doing something. Often, the silence is the doing.

Q3. What if they ask for advice straight away?

Sure, you can give it, but try first asking, "Do you want ideas, or do you just want me to listen?" That way, you're not serving up a full TED Talk when they were really just after a listening ear and a bit of breathing space.

Q4. How do I know when to step in with solutions?

If they're truly stuck, overwhelmed, or actually saying the words, "Can you help?" That's your cue. Even then, keep them in the driver's seat by asking, "What have you already tried?" or "What do you think might work?"

Q5. What's the difference between "holding space" and "holding the frame"?

Holding space is your calm presence, like opening the door and letting them walk in with whatever they're carrying. Holding the frame is what keeps the conversation from tipping into *your* agenda instead of theirs.

Q6. What if my young adult gets angry with me while I'm holding space?

It happens. In my family, they've become perceptive to my "coach mode" strategies, especially when I pivot from being fully drawn in to suddenly "holding space." They don't always like it. The trick is not to take it personally, even if it feels like a direct hit. Keep the frame steady, resist the urge to bite back, and circle back later when the temperature has dropped.

Q7. How do I encourage self-compassion without sounding preachy?

Share your own battle stories. Talk about the times you've gone ten rounds with your inner critic and what you're learning to do differently. If you can model it out loud, "No, wait, I'm not an idiot, I just made a mistake," you make it real, not theoretical.

Q8. Can I use these tools with younger children or other adults?

Yes. The principles of presence, curiosity, and non-judgement work across all ages and relationships. The language might change, but presence, curiosity, and kindness never go out of style.

Q9. What if I totally mess up and say the wrong thing?

Then you've successfully modelled that adults also have no idea what they're doing. Correct course; carry on.

Q10. What if they roll their eyes at me?

Consider it advanced-level communication for young adults. Eye rolls often mean *I hear you, but I'm not ready to admit it.*

ESPECIALLY FOR YOU

It's so easy to imagine that other parents have this whole thing figured out while we're the only ones quietly losing the plot. I promise you, they don't. No one's nailing it. If you think you've found a parent who is, please introduce me; I'd like to study them in the wild.

Parenting is relentless. Beautiful, yes, but relentless. The tools you try to teach your kids are often the same ones you'll need to hand back to yourself. None of us has them lined up like an emotional SWAT team waiting for deployment. What we have is practice—messy, repetitive, and humbling practice. That's what makes the difference. It's not about using the tools perfectly; it's about returning to them, even when yesterday was a disaster. What matters most are the small decisions to make connection a priority.

And yet, sitting beside your children, no matter how old they are, means feeling their pain too. That part is natural, but you also need to watch it carefully. There's a line between empathy and absorption, that moment when you stop saying, "Wow, that must be heavy," and start feeling it in your chest as though it belongs to you.

Psychologists call it "emotional contagion." I call it being a mom. It's when someone you love feels something so deeply that it starts affecting you, too. Their fear, sadness, or frustration almost fuses with your own before you've even realised that it's happening. In families, it's almost unavoidable. But separating what belongs to them from what's rising in you is vital because no one can help anyone if you're both sliding.

When your child is hurting, the pull to carry their pain is strong. Every instinct is to fix, soothe, or solve. And yet, when you do, it adds a quiet layer of responsibility for them too. They start trying to hold you together.

I'm not suggesting you hide what you're feeling, only that you don't wear it. Because when you do, it shifts the atmosphere in the entire home. The air changes, laughter feels forced, small irritations swell, and no one quite knows where it's safe to land. Everyone becomes a little smaller, a little more guarded, as if they're waiting for the atmosphere to settle before they can stretch again.

Parenting in real time, without a map or a guarantee, can feel like slow torture. You just want reassurance that they'll be okay. The truth is, that feeling doesn't disappear when they're grown. If anything, it intensifies. You might think you'll relax once they're adults. Not a chance. It's worse. The world they live in now feels more unpredictable, and the illusion of control slips further away.

So, you remind yourself: the bumps and bruises, the heartbreaks, the disappointments, and even the mistakes are their work now. This is where they learn to bend without breaking.

Your job? Let them. And there it is again.

I should have Mel Robbins on speed dial at this point, maybe even send her an invoice, but she's right. Let them flounder. Let them figure it out. Let them feel it. That's where the real growth and learning live.

That fierce protective streak never disappears. You'll still remember the name of the child who bit yours in nursery and occasionally wonder what he's doing now (hopefully not biting). That's the mother-bear instinct in all of us. It's what makes us nurturers and protectors. We'll love, care, and worry for them until our last breath. The trick is learning to do it from a healthy distance.

Sometimes, they'll still call with an "emergency." You'll hear the wobble in their voice and feel the old rescue reflex kick in. You'll want to fix it. But you'll also know that rescuing them now takes away the very thing they need most: the chance to realise they can handle it.

When you manage to hold back, even just a little, you'll start to see the foundation you've built together: all the crying, talking, repairing, and trying again. That's what steadies them when you're not there.

So, if you find yourself somewhere between holding on and letting go, take heart. None of us really knows what we're doing; we're all just learning how to love people without losing ourselves in the process.

FINAL THOUGHTS

So here we are, young adulthood complete. We spend years keeping them close, creating soft landings, and working for connection, then suddenly the work is to step back. If you think you are going to throw your arms up in celebration and move on, I'm here to tell you that this is not going to happen.

While they're figuring out the emotional work of adulting, we're learning to stay with our own emotions, to notice what's happening in us, stay rooted, and admit that this letting go hurts like hell. That honesty matters. It tells them that we're not just parents; we're people too, still learning, still stretching, and still letting go right alongside them.

What comforts me most now is realising that presence is still enough, even here. It just looks different. It's the kind of presence that steps back but doesn't disappear. It loosens its grip but keeps its heartbeat close. That's the presence our children carry with them, knowing that we're still here, loving them from just the right distance.

My challenge to you—and still to me—is to trust that the tools we've modelled will carry them further than our interference ever could. It's the difference between pulling them from the pool and standing at the edge saying, "I know you can swim, and I'll be right here if you need me."

It's not natural, this business of loosening our grip on the people we'd die to protect. Every part of me still wants to throw in a float. But I'm learning that the most powerful moments often happen when I don't.

Kahlil Gibran wrote that parents are the bows from which their children, as living arrows, are sent forth. Our work is not to aim for them but to steady ourselves, release the string, and let them fly. And as they do, we finally get to turn back toward our own lives, asking softly, *What now?*

That's kind of a scary question. Who are we when we're not holding everything together? What happens when we finally have the time and the quiet to listen to our own hearts? This time is about remembering what brings us alive.

It might feel strange at first, but there's so much waiting to be found. The growth we've modelled for them is the same growth we now get to live, right out in the open. As they watch, they'll see not just the mother who raised them but the woman who's still unfolding, proof that emotional growth doesn't end when the children leave home.

And if you're not there yet, you'll get there. Just keep doing the work in the meantime. It makes the transition into this next stage of growth so much easier. One day, your child will be standing right where you are now, watching their own kid stumble off with the map upside down, and they'll stop and think, *Oh, this is what she meant.* They'll remember that you trusted them to find their own way, and that memory will stay with them long after they've gone their own way.

FOR SKIM LOVERS

Whether you're glancing at this before work, revisiting after a long day, or wanting a quick pulse check on what matters most, here's your shortcut to staying emotionally present with your young adult, or the young adult you may one day have.

When navigating the emotions of a young adult, keep in mind...

You're still their anchor.

But now your job is less about holding them still and more about giving them room to find their own balance.

It's presence without intrusion.

Be close enough to notice, far enough to let them work through the moment, even when you could fast-track the solution.

The urge to step in is real.

You'll see emotional storms coming, disappointments, impulsive choices, moments where they trust the wrong person, and you'll want to soften the blow. Breathe. Let them test their own tools.

They grow most by using the tools, not borrowing yours.

That means giving them space to regulate their emotions, even if it looks messy or takes longer than you'd like.

Your modelling still matters.

The way you handle your own emotions teaches them as much as any advice you've ever given. Show them what it looks like to pause, listen, and choose your words carefully.

Silence can be powerful.

Sometimes the best support is sitting alongside them without fixing, tidying, or translating their feelings. It says, *I believe you can handle this.*

Boundaries are emotional safety nets.

It's not about rules for them, but limits for yourself. Boundaries keep you from steering their life while keeping the relationship strong.

This stage isn't just their growth spurt.

It's yours too. As they practise resilience, you practise patience. As they stretch into independence, you stretch into self-awareness.

THE TAKEAWAY:

Parenting young adults isn't about stepping out of the picture; it's about being the steady frame that holds the picture in place. You're not the whole story anymore, but you're still part of the reason it holds together. When they do look back, they'll remember not just what you said, but how you stayed present.

Part VI

Carrying It Forward

SMALL ACTS, LONG REACH

Have you ever noticed that the word "motion" sits right there in the middle of "emotion"? I only spotted that recently, and honestly, it blew my mind a little. It's a reminder that emotions are meant to move in, through, up, down, up again, and out.

When we know how we want to show up as parents and understand the value of that stance, our job becomes to help our children feel their emotions, name them, and recognise that the ups and downs are simply part of growing.

Which brings us full circle to what that growth has looked like for Michaela, Matthew, and Josh. Let's first acknowledge that they are truly the stars of this show. With all the emotional development, sibling drama, tears, laughter, and chaos, I'd like to think we've got all the makings of a BAFTA-winning family documentary, right here in these pages.

Josh's growth has always had volume. When he was little, his emotions had a way of spilling out and sweeping the rest of us along for the ride. I only have to think about the chain reaction of drama that could be heard across the school fields when he was fouled, or worse, when his team lost a game. Those big, unprocessed feelings had nowhere to land, and the rest of us were pulled right into the storm.

These days, the ripple looks different. When he feels himself tipping, he recognises it. When the pressure builds, he pauses and resets. Even better, he can put it into words: "Mom, I'm not skiving off work. I just need to do something different to clear my mind." That right there is emotional grounding and connection rolled into one.

Doing this work has shown me how much of my own stuff used to spill into his world. I found old, frayed feelings labelled *Not Good Enough* tucked into that old "Deal with Later" folder. Without meaning to, I tried to "make him enough" to make myself feel better. That's my work, not his. Still, when he drifts or coasts or just does the things teenage boys do, those old fears start circling. *What if he falls behind, what if he doesn't reach his potential, and what if the cracks in me surface in him?* The only reason I can see this pattern now is because I've done the work. When Josh senses my panic rising, he asks what I'm feeling and tells me how it lands on him. I don't always handle it gracefully; sometimes I wish I'd just stayed quiet, but it's real. And real, I've learned, is where connection happens.

We're still in the trenches of adolescence, which means plenty of peaks and troughs, but we level out faster now. Maybe it's because I stopped pretending to have it all figured out, or maybe because I started this work earlier than I did with Michaela and Matthew. Whatever it is, there are moments when Josh can read the room like a pro, spotting emotional undercurrents long before I do. Growth indeed.

Michaela's growth has its own shape. She was the first, and she'll tell you that any chance she gets. Fair enough. The eldest always gets the rough draft of their parents. I should know. When she was left out of the Fabulous Five, her feelings were written all over her face. She didn't hide from it; she sat in the ache, turned it over, and somehow made something steady out of it. Another mother said, "She's handled that amazingly." I held on to those words for years, repeating them back to her as proof that the work we do on ourselves shows up in our children, too.

Her teenage years were another story: raw, loud, sometimes unbearable. There were moments I thought we'd lost each other completely. But what came out of that wasn't distance; it was understanding. We both came through the fire a little scorched, a little wiser, and a lot more real.

Even now, as I write this book, we talk about it. How we could have done things differently. What we've learned. What we carry forward. And that "carry forward" is what I see in her now, in the way she pauses before reacting, in how she names what she's feeling and looks underneath it instead of running away. She's not afraid of the work anymore. She's lived through it. She's seen what it gives back.

Matthew's growth has been quieter, but no less powerful. For years, I mistook his silence for ease, thinking that still waters meant calm. Only later did I realise his quiet wasn't just layers; it was whole chapters I hadn't read. Through him, I'm learning a different kind of listening, the kind that happens in stillness. It hasn't come naturally; I'm a talker, and silence makes me itch. But I'm learning to let the pauses stretch long enough for him to find his rhythm.

His quiet has taught me patience, and that love can be steady even when words are few. For him, it's meant stepping into spaces that don't always feel comfortable. Sometimes he'll say, "I'm not good at explaining myself," and I remind him there's no right or wrong way to do it; there's just trying, learning, and growing together. My role is to stay near enough to encourage but far enough not to crowd. It's not neat or quick, and it doesn't look like my way. It's his, and that's what matters.

Watching Matthew emerge has been something I quietly marvel at. It's like watching light push through layers that were always there but hidden. And the only reason I can see it now is because I finally stepped aside and let him do the work. Love, I've realised, sometimes means loosening your grip so you can stand back and see who they become.

Of course, there's no "emotional growth exemption" for mothers. These days, when my feelings start to spiral, it's not unusual for one of the three to look at me and say, "What do you need right now, Mom?" The first time it happened, I almost laughed, partly out of pride and partly out of horror, because, well, that's my line.

I never sat them down and taught that phrase. They learned it because it's what I've always asked of them. What they expect now, and rightly so, is for me to pause and check in with myself. That little pause gives me a moment to notice what's really going on, whether I'm reacting out of habit or actually responding to what's been said. Most of the time, that check-in leaves me calmer and more present, which, frankly, works out better for everyone. Apparently, there's real value in my doing my own emotional homework. It turns out that everyone benefits when I don't skip class.

None of this happened overnight. It started with a deliberate decision to put emotional understanding right at the centre of our family life, squeezed somewhere between the dirty laundry and the half-drunk cups of tea. It's not written on a poster stuck to the fridge or listed under "family rules." It's just what we try to do. It's my hope—no, it's my belief—that they will carry all of this into their adult lives. That one day they'll sit across from someone they love, words hanging sharp in the air, and instead of snapping back, they'll pause, breathe, and remember what we practised here. They may hold children of their own and know that feelings aren't chaos to contain but clues to follow.

I don't know about you, but I'm planning on being around to see all of this, reminding myself that the way they teach, model, and grow with their own families is going to be their journey alone (and I already know this is going to be hard, and I'll probably have to bite my tongue). Hopefully, with a little self-restraint and a lot of deep breathing, I'll remember that my role is to love, encourage, and enjoy the privilege of still being part of their lives.

CONCLUSION

In learning to understand and process emotions within our family, I have returned to a question time and time again: *What kind of parent do I want to be when emotions fill the room?*

When life was at its busiest and I was running on auto-pilot, my answer would have been "calm." What mother doesn't long for calm amid the chaos of motherhood? For me, it's right up there with chocolate, another thing I reach for when the wheels start to come off. But if I'd stopped to really think about the question, I would have realised that calm was only my knee-jerk answer. Thinking it through properly takes time and emotional energy, two things I didn't have much of back then.

In coaching, the easiest response to a difficult question is usually, "I don't know." And sometimes that's true; we really don't. But sometimes, "I don't know" is just a way of saying, *I don't want to look too closely at that yet,* because we know that if we do, something inside us might start to shift. That kind of honesty can feel like stepping into cold water.

Still, when you stay with the question long enough and resist the urge to move on too quickly, you start to see yourself a little more clearly. That's when the real work begins. And I'm not talking about some polished version of growth that belongs on a podcast or a vision board. I'm talking about the quiet, private kind that unfolds when you pay attention to what you most value.

That question that has followed me for years: *What kind of parent do I want to be when emotions fill the room?* I used to come at it like an exam I might fail, scribbling down answers, changing them, and crossing them out again. Some days I still do. But slowly, I've come to see it less as something to solve and more as something to live by.

When emotions are high and I can feel myself reacting instead of responding, I try to ask: *What is it about this version of me that doesn't feel right? Why does it matter so deeply? How would I like to meet this moment differently next time?* Those tiny questions have become the scaffolding for how I parent, shaky at first, but steadying over time. Sometimes my answer is, "I don't know." But when I start to see the version of me reacting without a clear foundation (let's just say, the Lewis Hamilton version), I realise it's time to get back on track.

It took time to see it, but I know now the kind of mother I want to be when emotions fill the room. I want to be the one who doesn't shrink away. The one who can sit in it, steady enough for everyone to stay real without feeling wrong. I want to listen longer, even when it's messy or inconvenient, and resist the pull to fix. I want to be able to offer safety over solutions, and steadiness over control. Most of all, I want to remember that my child's feelings aren't aimed at me; they're a glimpse into *them*.

Writing this down turned vague intentions into something solid. It's a reminder I reach for when words are rising too fast. It's made me a parent who can hold the full weight of her own emotions as well as theirs, and that kind of steadiness is what gives them the courage to face their own.

When I began this book, I told you about my resignation letter, the one I drafted in my head when I thought I wasn't cut out for this job. If toddler tantrums and teenage storms were going to keep coming, perhaps I could just step down gracefully.

But I didn't resign. I re-signed to presence—to showing up as I am, with all my learning and fumbling, with no illusions of perfection or fixing every problem, and certainly without aspiring to be the mythical "other mother" my daughter once wished for, because this work matters. The rewards of it are already taking root.

While my children's emotions have been taking shape, as they've navigated the familiar ups and downs of growing up, I've been growing up too. I've learned to stay steadier in the messiness of human connection, not only in our home but also with friends, colleagues, and with myself. Practising the pause, learning to listen longer than feels comfortable, and finding language for repair have spilt into every corner of my life.

Do I still falter, fall, and even berate myself because I "should know better"? Absolutely. When that happens, I remind myself that some of my greatest growth has come out of those very slips and stumbles.

Wherever you find yourself, whether it's in the thick of toddler chaos, outside a teenager's locked door, or waving goodbye to a young adult, keep walking the path. The rewards will come. Your children will grow with a stronger sense of safety and connection, and you will grow too, into a steadier, truer version of yourself. Most of all, you'll find a family rooted in emotional depth, held together by trust, resilience, and a connection that carries on long after the noise of childhood has quieted.

The real gift in all of this isn't the tidy house or the Christmas traditions we pretend not to care about but would riot if we lost. It's the messy, miraculous act of sticking around and figuring it out together.

So, keep going. Keep practising. Keep picking up the thread, even when it feels frayed. One day, you'll look back and see that what felt like small, ordinary moments were the very ones that held it all together. And if you ask me, that's a story worth telling.

ACKNOWLEDGEMENTS

For as long as I can remember, friends and family have told me, "You should write a book." I never quite believed them. My English teacher at school certainly didn't, and as a life-long in-the-box thinker, I took her word for it. It turns out she was wrong.

Somewhere between COVID lockdowns and too much overthinking, I signed up for online coaching with Alison du Toit. Alison helped me rediscover what I had quietly buried: the part of me that still had something to say. She showed me that motherhood had not erased me but shaped me, and that my voice had only been waiting for encouragement to speak. Thank you, Alison, for helping me believe in myself again.

That new spark of courage led me to Optimus Coaching Academy and Ruth Kudzi, whose wisdom, integrity, and ongoing investment in her students created a ripple effect I still feel today. Ruth, your belief in people does not end when the course does, and that is rare. I am grateful for your support, your example, and the way you have gathered a community that keeps growing together.

Through Ruth, I met Isabelle Fielding, whose gentle encouragement and kindness made me feel like I could do this. Somehow, I believed her. Thank you, Isabelle.

Through the same network, I met Sarah Bramall and Rebecca Daniel, who took a chance on me and invited me into their world. Working alongside you both helped me grow in confidence and clarity. You gave my voice a platform, and through that, I began to understand the true value of connection. Living that value brought my purpose to life, and for that, I will always be thankful.

Through the Coaching Catalyst Collective, I met Laura Presland, who became a close friend and mentor. You have walked beside me through the highs, the doubts, and the occasional crises of confidence. You have nudged me forward when I was tempted to retreat. Your GSD girls have been my sounding board, my cheerleaders, and my companions over coffee and cinnamon buns. I do not only want to thank you all; I want to say *we did it*. You know what that means.

To Paola Cringle from the I of M, thank you for arriving in my life at exactly the right time. You continue to push me beyond what feels safe and remind me to keep expanding. I look forward to many more collaborations ahead.

To Jason and Cecilia Hilkey of Happily Family: You made me see that dreams can become reality, and that we do not have to be somebody to achieve them. Cecilia, your gentle authenticity reached across the virtual screen and many miles of ocean, from the USA to London, and somehow said, "Come, I'll show you how." And you did. I am forever grateful to both of you for the opportunity to write and be part of a bestselling book collaboration. That experience was my true entry into the world of writing, and I will always be thankful for it.

And then there is Ann Sheybani of Summit Press Publishing. Who would have thought that a publisher could have such heart? Your kindness and encouragement have steadied me when doubt crept in. You helped me see what is normal, reminded me that this process is human, and you quickly recognised my need for deadlines. Thank you for keeping me focused and on track while also allowing me space to breathe. The balance has been perfect.

And finally, to the main characters of this book: Neil, Michaela, Matthew, and Josh. None of this would exist without you.

Neil, thank you for reading and rereading every draft, often more times than anyone should. It feels fitting that this book arrives as we celebrate thirty years of marriage. You have seen me in the seasons when I felt invisible and reminded me, gently but firmly, that what I was doing mattered. When I doubted myself, your quiet belief steadied me. This book carries your calm strength.

To Michaela, Matthew, and Josh, thank you for allowing me to share our story in all its imperfect beauty. You have always been willing to let our moments become lessons for others. Thank you for growing with me, forgiving me when I stumbled, and letting me learn out loud. Parenting you has been the greatest education of my life. It is not something I do to you; it is something we do together. We are still figuring it out, all of us, and I would not trade this ride for anything.

ABOUT THE AUTHOR

LEONORA FOUND is an accredited Life Coach and Emotions Coaching Practitioner dedicated to helping families integrate emotional intelligence and connection into their everyday lives. Drawing on her professional training and personal experiences, she guides parents to slow down, listen, and respond to one another with greater understanding, compassion, and care.

Her work emerged from the realization that nurturing our inner world is not selfish but essential for the well-being of those we love. Through her coaching and writing, she empowers others to rediscover the quiet strength of emotional awareness and its potential to transform not only family relationships but also our self-perception.

With a background in Industrial Psychology and Communications, Leonora blends psychological insight with down-to-earth humour and honesty, making her writing deeply relatable. Her work reminds us that emotional growth is an ongoing journey, one we practice together.

BONUS:
WHEN YOU SAY "I'M FINE"

You've been the Steady One. The Absorber. The One Who Keeps It Together.

But who's holding you?

This short companion guide goes deeper into the invisible emotional roles we slip into as parents—the ones that feel noble until they start costing us our peace, our presence, and our honest connection with ourselves.

Inside, you'll find:

- The 5 most common emotional roles parents carry (and why we grab onto them)
- What's really happening when you automatically say "I'm fine"
- Guided questions to help you recognise which roles you've been playing—and at what cost
- A short check-in practice you can return to when you need it
- If you've ever felt exhausted by your own okayness, this guide will help you find what's underneath it.

Access your free copy here:
http://leonorafound.com/resources/